A Flower in the Snow

A Flower in the Snow

The Journals and Poems of Another Overcomer

QuYahni Denise Lewis

Copyright © 1994-2010 by QuYahni Denise Lewis.

Library of Congress Control Number: 2010908909
ISBN: Hardcover   978-1-4535-2346-9
              Softcover   978-1-4535-2345-2
              Ebook   978-1-4535-2347-6

All rights reserved. No part of this book may be reproduced or transmitted in any form or by any means, electronic or mechanical, including photocopying, recording, or by any information storage and retrieval system, without permission in writing from the copyright owner.

This book was printed in the United States of America.

To order additional copies of this book, contact:
Xlibris Corporation
1-888-795-4274
www.Xlibris.com
Orders@Xlibris.com
81351

CONTENTS

Chapter One—Journal

- Purple Rooftops (February 1980) 15
- History 21
- Stuff Got Deeper Along the Way 24
- Double Belt Whoopin' and Mopstick Beatdown 30
- Daddy 36
- Some Robert, Some Jessie 39
- Everywhere I Go 46
- The Burning 49
- I Knew It Was Time to Go 57
- Suicide Attempt 69
- Edith 73
- The Way He Loved Me (7 Abortions Part I) 77
- A Rational Conversation about Child Support 81
- Every Rose Has Thorns 87
- Number Six (7 Abortions, Part II) 92
- It Was April 11, 1999 95
- Get Ready 99
- Hope To Get Over 101
- Seven Abortions Part III 103
- Wisdom of Dawn 104
- The ACS Case, Part I 106
- What I Wanted to Say 118
- The ACS Case, Part II 120
- 2006 126
- The ACS Case, Part III 128
- From Shoni 134

Chapter 2—Poetry

Let Me Write 137
Skin Deep 140
He Made Me 141
Holding On 143
Abril, Mil Novicientos Ochenta Y Tres 145
Nina Simone 146
My Sister Doesn't Cry 148
A Flower In The Snow 150
Pity Party 153
Little Girl 158
¿Hasta El Fuego? 160
Remembering (Holding On Part 2) 162
They Said 163
When JC Comes 164
Black Sunday Dawning 165
Rebirth of a Sista 167
Who Knows 169
Beautiful 170
January 2009 (Random Thought 1) 171
The Condition of My Body As I Try
   Not to Lose My Mind (Random Thought 2) 173
Not-Life, Death, & the Resurrection 175
Child of The King (Chosen One) 177
To Love (A Song) 179
Shelter 181
Para Mi Domi 182
Friendly Fire 184
Loving U 185
Strange Connection 186
The Best Love Yet (Para Mi Domi Part 2) 188
Misty 189
I Forgot To Tell You Somethin' 191
Hearing from God 193
This Simple Melody 195
If I Was Blind 197
With Me (Para Mi Domi, Part 3) 198
The End 200

Statistics on Sexual Abuse 201
Statistics Surrounding Child Sexual Abuse 202
Finding Healing 205

Much Gratitude and Thanks To 207
Special Acknowledgments 209
Bibliography 211

For . . .

Daddy, Abba, Jesucristo, Mi Vida, Mi Mundo, Mi Cielo,
my everything—I love You. I pray this brings You much glory.
I know You'll never stop teaching me to love . . .

Para Mi Domi, Boobah, Lah-Lah, Moo-Moo, y Ju-C;
I love you on and on and on . . .

For every man, woman, boy, and girl who has ever
experienced misuse, neglect, and self-abuse . . .

And to those who did offend—you are forgiven . . .

Prelude

She was a little white girl with long, dirty-blonde hair that really looked dirty, wearing a dingy sheath that one could tell once was white, no shoes, insipid face, body walking dead. At first indoors, a building with no windows, condemned, appearing ravaged by fire.

She met her abductor there, a white man, tall, slim, handsome, straw-blond crew cut. He was not forceful, she did not resist. He led her out to another desolate place, a gas station, maybe it once was. A rural area with a wide tree-lined street that disappeared over a bizarrely steep hill. The sky was hoary, everything gray, but the trees verdant and beautiful; there were no other people, only she and her abductor.

She followed, walking dead. He laid her down upon the ground. He placed her right arm—her "write" arm—upon a short broken single strip of railroad track. He had a hammer and nine-inch nails. He drove them into her arm in three different places—her wrist, her inner elbow, and her forearm; she heard a voice say, "Fight! Don't just lie there, you don't have to let this happen!" She did not know where the voice came from, it sounded around—not in—her. She did not listen, she did not flinch, she felt no pain; impassive face and quitter's mind held her prisoner, convinced her that she could not win.

She waited for nails to the other arm, they did not come. He stood straight and asked her, "What color paper would you like?" She did not respond; again she heard him, "I'm not going anywhere until you tell me what color paper you want." She lay unresponsive, still awaiting the drive of the next set of nails.

She was suddenly facedown, arm secured to the track, still; she could not respire, too done-in to reposition herself, yet trying to move.

Then she was in her bed, on her face, no nails in her arm, but unable to move; she struggled onto her right side. Her abductor lie next to her, between she and her husband, still going on about paper, her back, to him, face mashed in pillow, she picked mild visions of her frail consciousness, they were like flickers in the dark, visions of brilliantly boxed watercolor-painted-square-cut paper, varying hues of blue or green with flecks and streams of silver or gold, torpidly her mouth muttered her choice, he went off to get it . . .

—*A Dream of Me on December 31, 2005*

Chapter One—Journal

Purple Rooftops (February 1980)

"I HAFTA GO NOW. I was only s'posed to be goin' to the store. I'm gonna git in trouble."

"Okay, go ahead."

He motions for me to pass under his arm. His hand is on the banister, and he is blocking the stairway, so I have to go that way. His face isn't nice anymore. I try to go. Smooth like capoeira, his left arm goes around my neck and pulls my back to his chest. He puts that hand over my mouth; that hand that only minutes before had handed me peppermint balls and change. His right hand—the one that is resting on the banister—goes to my neck. There is a knife. He whispers in my ear. "If you scream, I will cut your throat. Walk up the stairs."

There are two short flights of stairs leading to the roof. He still holds me to his chest, his knife resting against my throat. He opens the door to the roof and leads me out into the purple blackness. He turns me toward him and puts me up against a wall. We are right behind the roof door.

I remember times when Edith told me "I'ma whoop yo' ass when you git home." I remember palpitations and tremors and mind racing in anticipation of the beating to come. I remember being afraid of *that*. On this rooftop, there is fear, but there is hope that I have no control over that stands beside it. The sky is purple and the moon is big and full. I keep my eyes on purple sky and big moon and I plead, although not with this man.

"I wanna go home. "

"Shut the eff up. "

"I wanna go home. Please, God, I wanna go home. Please let me go home. "

"Shut the eff up before I cut yo' throat! "

"I wanna go home. Oh God, please, I wanna go home."

"Shut up."

But I can't. I see only his teeth. His dark skin is camouflaged by black pea coat and black wool cap and purple night sky. For twenty-five years after that I won't remember what he looks like. When I tell this story, I will be able to make out nearly every feature of his face. But at this moment on the roof, it is just angry teeth and slits-for-eyes as I look from purple sky and its moon to his face and then back to the sky, the moon. And I plead with God to take me home. Whatever home is.

He opens my coat and puts his free hand on my breasts. He pinches them. They are small—they are brand new; puberty, I think, is slowly becoming my friend. The cold February air, however, is not. The twin pubescent newness between my neck and belly responds against my will to its crisp icy touch. The shiny rayon turtleneck I wear has a run through its silver, red, and white horizontal stripes, going down the right breast. It was a target for my peers' jokes earlier that day at school. He is touching my nipples, and all I can think about is the run in my shirt. He fumbles with his pants. He gives me instructions. I nod my head.

A few seconds of what seemed forever and there is a rush. It is bitter and warm. A little while, and then another rush. Only thicker. And spurty. It is bitter, too, only not so hot. I know—I know that the first rush—that is pee. And then there is the second one. Semen. To vomit would cost me for sure. The moon is so pretty. Pretty purple sky.

"I wanna go home."

He tells me to count to 100.

"If you stop before you get to 100, I will come back and kill you."

"One, two, three, four, five, six, seven . . . eight, nine . . ." The sound of his running feet disappears down the stairs. Hope assuages fear; I run down the steps and knock on the first door I see; the door by the stairs where he put his hand over my mouth.

I bang on the door.

"Who is it?"

It is a woman's voice. My heart leaps.

"Somebody please let me in! A man took me to the roof and made me suck his prick!" (I learned that word in a black man/white man joke book.) The door flies open and behind it stands a tiny woman; a woman as small as ten-year-old me. I rush into her arms, bury my face in her chest, and cry.

I AM SITTING IN THE PADDY WAGON, watching the police stop every black man wearing a pea coat. I am going numb with no one to talk to.

"I said 'dark-skinned, black hat, pea coat,' not 'light-skinned, glasses, pea coat.'"

I share this only with myself. I am forgotten for the moment as officers use my misfortune to compound the pain of living an existence rife with racist inflections that dig deep into the manhood of a people still fighting for a chance; the throbbing of which probably drove the dark figure that singed my insides with his demons tonight.

Edith is waiting at the precinct. I hug her. It is the first and only time (except for the first of the month) that I am ever glad to see her; to my recollection, anyway. She hugs me, too, I think, and acts really concerned. I think she is.

The sketch artist shows me the drawing. It is the description that I gave him, but I don't know who in hell is on this paper. I can't remember his face. I just know he's real dark and wearing all black and has a nice smile. I don't tell them about the nice smile. I don't tell them that I followed willingly into the building and up the stairs. I lie. I tell them he followed me. I am scared they will blame me. I already do.

There are questions, mug shots, and lineups. Countless pages of young Black faces, young Latino faces, beautiful hurting faces. I learn what the word *ejaculation* means. And I am already numb. I am good at going numb. After each time, it just gets easier and easier. And even though, this time, it happened with a stranger, it is just as easy.

We're *home* now. Okay, we're in our building and we're walking toward our first-floor apartment. The super's wife is on her way upstairs. Edith stops her to give her the news.

"Don't let your daughter out of the house—a man just took Denise up to the roof and made her suck his d**k! "
"Oh my God! Where did this happen? "
"Right up on The Concourse—the building right on the corner up there! "
"Oh sh*t! "
"Yeah, we jus' came back from the precinct!"

More bits and pieces of my self-esteem go crumbling to the floor. We go inside. I just keep my head up and forward. Numb. Nobody knows.

Edith lets me sleep in her bed that night. She lets me watch TV until I fall asleep sucking on the lone lollipop I purchased before it all went down. I pack away her indiscretion in an overstuffed storage bin that I didn't know I had; a bin that would one day explode and make a very big mess.

When I get to school the next morning, my teacher speaks with me in private about the events of the night before. So do the kids on the block when I get home that afternoon (alone again, naturally). Although not so pleasantly; not so privately.

"I heard that a man took you up on the roof and made you . . ."

DETECTIVES AND MUG SHOTS, lineups, and neighborhood drive-throughs produce nothing. Sometimes the neighborhood drive-throughs include other girls who had been sexually assaulted. We all share our stories. Well, everyone except me. I just can't get myself to tell those girls what that man did to me. One girl tells us she answered the door for a stranger and he pushed his way into the apartment. Another girl says it happened in the park. The same guy raped another girl along with her sister. Still others have similar stories; all were raped and, somehow, it all seems so much less shameful than what happened to me. None of them make mention of anyone peeing in their mouths.

My first set of detectives is the proverbial "Good Cop, Bad Cop." Bad Cop treats me like a perp.

They come to visit me at the babysitter's. They have more questions and they want me to reenact the incident. I am walking by Bad Cop during my reenactment and I trip over her foot. I say sorry and she gives me a "look." She is tall and big and black and menacing from the moment she walks in the door. Good Cop is tall but quiet, soft, and pale. He doesn't say much. Bad Cop gives all the instructions.

"Show me how you walked when you went into the building looking for help."

This makes no sense to me. What is this going to prove? I walk by, trying to do what Bad Cop says and trip over her foot again.

"If you step on my foot one more time, you're gonna have some problems."

I'm done after that. I am nervous and I can't think straight. I've already lied about looking for help. I didn't know that this man that I met on the street on my way to buy some candy was going to take me up on a roof. He told me he had a bike he wanted to sell. I went with him willingly into that building because I really thought he was gonna take me to see it. I wasn't afraid until we were standing by the stairs on the top floor, when his eyes went dark and his smile disappeared. Maybe Bad Cop knows this. Maybe she's related to someone who looks like the sketch artist's rendering. Maybe it was her baby boy who let loose in me on that pretty violet night.

I get new detectives after that; two nice white guys who buy me lunch and give me pocket change when they drop me off after our visits to the precinct and the courthouse. After a couple of weeks, no detectives come to pick me up anymore. And I don't even ask why. I just keep living. Just as I did after Uncle D. And Ma Hattie's boys (they liked to lay me on top of them while they sat in chairs, pretend they were sleeping, and gyrate beneath me). And Cousin Leo.

"Wanna see something? "
"Yeah! Out it comes. "
"There's this white stuff in it. You want me to show you how to make it come out? "
"Yeah."

Every day while I was six years old—for as long as Leo was living in our house—I did what he taught me until the white stuff came out. He never touched me. But I spent every afternoon after school touching him. And I really didn't mind. I called him my boyfriend.

Something in me knew it was wrong. But it became normal to me. I don't know why I started liking it; why I began to look for invitations. It would become my story for nearly two decades. It was who I was.

You wanna play house? became the prelude to make-out sessions with groups of cousins, episodes in stairwells with whomever was willing, kissing tiny penises just because they asked me to, hiding in closets with boys or girls—whoever made the offer, playing *Run-Catch-And-Kiss* in the snow, hiding behind mounds, availing myself to hands and lips and hips; and I was smiling, always smiling. They would laugh while they groped or ground. They would wait their turn. And I would keep smiling.

Out in the open, I was Four-Eyes. I was funny to look at, fun to tease. And I wore it willingly—I knew they needed me. I longed for the invisibility of the mounds of snow, the darkness of the closets, the places where I reigned, where my body commanded all attention. Where Four-Eyes and funny-looking didn't exist. I always knew, no matter where I was, I would have a place. At first, I would be Four-Eyes. But I would always become something to hold; even if only for a little while. Even if it was just body parts. Even if it wasn't real. And that was enough.

History

THESE ARE MY STORIES, but there are some other people you should know. I have changed some names, not all, just some. And some I don't mention at all.

Edith is my biological mother. Her maiden name is McClain. Her father was George McClain, but we called him "Daddy."

Edith is one of twelve brothers and sisters. As I write this, there are only six of them left, including Edith. Louis was Edith's husband. They were married in February of 1967. I had three siblings—two brothers and a sister: Harold, Nilda, and Jessie. Harold was the eldest, I am seven years younger than him; Nilda is two years younger than me; and Jessie was a year younger than Nilda. Harold and I had different fathers, different from each other, and different from Nilda's and Jessie's dad. Nilda is definitely Louis's child; Jessie, I'm not so sure. Harold and Jessie are gone . . . dead . . . but not in that order.

I was born in December of 1969. Louis's name is on my birth certificate, as it should be, because he accepted and cared for me; he really loved me. But my biological father is a mystery in the McClain family. He's a Puerto Rican man; so I'm a half-sie. I found that out when I was twenty-six years old. I'm not sure if I am at liberty to say how he knew my mother. Hopefully, if I can, I will have said so in a way that brings her no shame before these stories end.

I wish I could tell you about Louis. I wish I knew more. I have at least three memories: one of three-year-old-me performing impromptu dances for him to music only I could hear. We were in our living room in our one-bedroom apartment on Kelly Street in The Bronx. Edith was there. She sat in a corner on one side of the room; Louis sat on the twin bed that was on the other side, near the window. It was at the end of his workday, his face tired and worn, skin ashy, head hanging low with fatigue. Edith's face was hard to read. It was sad, maybe confused, maybe complacent. But in this memory, I paid little attention to her. I was dancing for Louis and I had real joy. That, I remember well.

There is another memory; Louis is sitting in our living room, only the walls look darker; there is no light but that emitted of an average-size fish tank. He is sitting on something I can't identify. There's really no furniture in this room—just odds and ends and wide-open space. I am dancing, again. Edith is in the kitchen. Harold is in the living room with Louis and me. There are no voices, only heads hanging low and tired. But I am all joy.

There is another memory still. I am in a church—an old country church—I am in the back and a service seems to have just ended. I see Nilda, she's about two years old, and she is wearing a frilly yellow dress. She is in the arms of a grown-up that I don't know. She and this grown-up are at the front of the church. I look and I see a big rectangular box; it, too, is at the front of the church. It's a pretty box—it has pillows and frills and satin and lace inside. Louis is in that box, lying on top of all the pillows, frills, and lace. His eyes are closed. He looks tired. Somehow I know that I won't be doing any more dances for him.

Life changed after that.

People say I was with Louis before he died; Harold and I were with him, they say. They say he was murdered and we saw the whole thing. I don't remember; I have tried—I have created visions in my mind based on the information they gave me. He was stabbed about the head repeatedly . . . he was beat about the head repeatedly . . . Harold and I were in the backseat . . . He drove us home . . . the ambulance came for him . . . he died in the hospital . . . I try to this day, but I don't recall any of these things.

There are other stories about Louis . . . Edith . . . some say he used to beat her . . . some say she cheated on him . . . so he beat her . . . some say she really loved him . . . but I remember the boyfriend moving in not too long after Louis died . . . along with some of the uncles and aunts and cousins . . . all in our one-bedroom apartment . . . Edith spent all the insurance money on the boyfriend . . . that's what they say . . . I think she spent it on all of them . . . along with her dignity and self-respect.

Anyway, I need to move on. To the story, I mean.

Stuff Got Deeper Along the Way

My big brother Harold worked as an usher at the movie theaters on pre-David-Dinkins-Forty-Second Street. I was twelve years old in the summer of 1982, when he told me to come downtown to see some free movies. I waited in the outer lobby area of one of the theaters. I was wearing my sailor suit—short white tie-front pullover top with electric blue polka dots and matching miniskirt, high-heeled, camel-colored espadrilles, and white sailor cap. But the Coke bottle-bottomed lenses in my glasses always killed my look. Nobody noticed my "sexy" except me . . . and men three times my age . . .

They saw differently. They walked by, they looked, they stopped. Lusty smiles lingered on my legs and crawled up my thighs. Scared, but tingling, I smiled, too . . .

Harold finally came for me, narrowly missing my convo with a passing admirer. He was still on duty, so he took me inside, sat me down in a triple feature and said he would be back soon. On this Forty-Second Street, you got kung fu or porn. There were bodies moving—arms and feet flailin' across the screen. There were moans and jolts, but it was not kung fu . . .

I sat in the dark surrounded by scattered cases of masturbation. Harold left me to watch *Uncle Someone-or-other* and *A King Dick Cartoon*. More notes for my already clogged mental erotica; I'd been collecting from Hustler, Playboy, other hardcore magazines and eight-track audio porn since I was four . . .

DURING THE SUMMER OF 1977, Edith left me with a lady named Ms. Betsy. She was a friend that Edith knew from Bryant Avenue. She had two sons and a daughter. The elder son's name was John, the other son, who was the youngest of the three, was nicknamed Rabbit. I don't remember the daughter's name, but I remember watching through their front window one day her very pregnant body as she dressed. She had a ton of stretch marks on her belly. It was scary and intriguing all at once.

Ms. Betsy had moved to Vyse Avenue, just one block parallel to Bryant. She had a Latino boyfriend whose voice and name I never heard. Back then, everybody who wasn't Black or White was Puerto Rican and no one ever bothered to find out where they really came from.

Ms. Betsy's son Rabbit used to mess with me whenever I spent the night at their street level apartment on Bryant Avenue. He and a friend always found opportunity to rub up on me; it was usually the prelude to a game of basketball. It was at that apartment that Ms. Betsy's boyfriend first messed with me, too.

I was five years old. I was sleeping one evening in Rabbit's room. Ms. Betsy's boyfriend came into the room, woke me gently, and put a nickel in my hand. Then he put his face there. It didn't hurt like the other things I'd experienced. The tingles that I had come to know shortly after my uncle D's attempt to penetrate me came rushing in,[1] wrestling with the truth in me that warned that this thing that went down between grown-ups and me just wasn't right.

Two years later, not soon after they had moved to Vyse Avenue and Edith had dropped me there with no explanation and no word of when she would return, Ms. Betsy's boyfriend paid another visit to me in the night. Same scenario . . . he came softly, with offerings of silence, small change, and pleasure that I could not understand.

---

[1] pp.34-35

I tried to pull him on top of me. I didn't care what he did; I needed someone to hold me; a body to connect with mine on purpose and in agreement with me; because he wasn't hurting me, I thought that he wanted me. But what he was doing felt separate and strange; like I wasn't a part of it. I was seven years old and, already, I was trying to manipulate—and not trying to stop—this wrong touch; it was right for as long as it took them to find what they were looking for, if it made them desire me.

Ms. Betsy's boyfriend didn't want to lie on top of me. He rested there for a moment, much too short of my appeasement, and then went back to what he had started. It was soon done and never repeated. No need to warn me to keep silent; it was already embedded . . . it was my secret life . . . the one that was given to me that I would never have asked for and could certainly have done without. But I was already in deep and I wasn't coming out for a long, long time.

THERE WAS A BLACKOUT THAT SUMMER. I was in the bathtub when everything went dark. I was content to continue my bath that way, but Ms. Betsy shooed me out of the tub and made me get dressed and go outside with her, the boyfriend, Rabbit, and the family German Shepherd.

The block was live. Boricua was everywhere, peppered with Afro-Blackness, battery-operated boom boxes were pumping and the Latino and R&B flavor of that era spilled out onto the streets. I was fascinated by the magic of the night; how everyone seemed to embrace the darkness and make it a party; people were united, drinking beer looted from several corner stores (when the lights went out, everything was fair game), smoking weed and laughing merrily. Everyone, even those we did not know, seemed to be family. I ran up and down the block, was all-up in grown-ups faces—an act that would normally get me slapped down and punished, but went unnoticed because everyone was caught up in the atmosphere. I played mostly with the older Latino children—the teenage girls—who adored me and had long before this evening adopted me as their own. I was like their mascot and, on that night, there seemed to be extra special love. I was glad I had abandoned my bath. That was the best time I had at Ms. Betsy's.

Harold came for me right before summer ended. I don't know if Edith sent him or if he noticed my long absence and decided to pick me up. Either way, I was met with no-welcome from Edith. We were living someplace new, again[2], in the basement with the superintendent of the building, Edith's latest temporary boyfriend (she had at least four in between breakups with Charlie[3]; but she somehow always ended up back with him). She was watching television when Harold and I walked in, and only looked up long enough to fling an emotionless "Hi," my way; no real eye contact, no queries about my summer. I knew from that moment that she had not intended to see me again.

Courtlandt Avenue and 151st Street was the new place. I had new boys to do nasty things with, and even a girl this time. Shortly after my return, the super/temporary boyfriend gave us an apartment on the fifth floor. My new school had the usual bullies, gropers, and mockers to whom my poor dress and unkempt hair were a magnet. If not for my good grades and love of writing, I would have had nothing to look forward to at school.

MY COURTLANDT AVENUE MEMORIES are pretty much the same as all the rest. Some relatives taught Jessie how to smoke weed when he was only five years old. One time, they left a joint on the dresser and I sat in the window and puffed it until it was gone. I was waiting for whatever it was that made my brother and my aunts and uncles giggle and act like little kids, but it never came. I didn't realize until I was a teenager and tried to smoke again (and still didn't get what I was looking for) that it was because

---

[2] When I was between the ages of four and thirteen, we changed residences a total of thirteen times, not including short stays w/ friends in between apartments. My mother only paid the rent when we moved in and we stayed until we got evicted. As an adult, I would emulate this behavior, not being evicted, but living with several different friends and family members until they were tired of me and I was able to find and keep my own place

[3] Charlie was Edith's boyfriend; he was the one who moved in with us shortly after Louis died

I hadn't inhaled. I didn't know how and I was scared I would choke to death if I sucked smoke back into my throat.

I wonder what Edith was thinking during all of this, if she knew. My most prominent visions are of her sitting on her messy bed in front of a black and white TV, focused and chomping on a Hostess cupcake.

MY FIRST SEXUAL ENCOUNTER WITH A GIRL happened shortly after my rescue from Ms. Betsy's house. Her name was Lavera. I was almost eight and she was four years my senior. She touched, she taught me to touch, we did this often.

I wish I could say that Lavera was different than the boys. In her bedroom, when no one was around, she was kind and made me forget that what we did was wrong. The gentleness and wanting me again and again made it worth the risk, but it was a tenderness reserved only for those times. In front of her brothers[4], and others, she joined in the scoffs; she initiated some unkindness; I was her last choice as friend.

A few years later, a boy named Noonie heard that I had said that I would never French kiss because I thought it was nasty. He would give me my first in the fall of 1982. My grandfather would give me my second that winter.[5] The following spring, my first real boyfriend, Dennis, often kissed me as Ms. Betsy's boyfriend did. He was fifteen.

When I was sixteen, my boyfriend Greg made the mistake of telling me that I was boring in bed. By then, I had been with Pretty Ricky[6]. He had taught me well in that he made me spend all my time pleasing him and I knew nothing else, really. So I did have *skills*, but I was afraid to expose them to others for fear of appearing "used." But being called boring sparked an even greater fear: rejection.

So I gathered all my tricks and took them to every show. For the next ten years I would be a circus monkey. I convinced myself that my witchcraft, my love-potion thighs, my spell-casting lips, my voodoo-doll eyes, would

---

4   Jounie was one of Lavera's brothers - pp. 46-47
5   p.37
6   pp. 56-67

shift the stars and make love happen for me. I thought it would come from down there, that one of them would fall in and never escape again.

And some did just that. They would get stuck in the image of me and I would listen to the raspy messages they left on my answering machine, I would suck my teeth and roll my eyes while I scantily dressed my way out the door to pick up the next piece. I would take those pieces and create the one man, that's what my subconscious believed, but they were all just pieces that wouldn't gel—pieces of them, and me. I spent a lot of time playing . . . telling them that I loved them . . . bemusing and inveigling . . . showering them with fake tears that always reeled them back in. I wanted them never to go away . . . I needed them.

Years later, I found myself with so many of them still inside of me, every day God painfully digging in and peeling away what was left of them so that I could be whole again, leaving a flaming sword guarding the place, just in case.

Double Belt Whoopin' and Mopstick Beatdown

Journal Entry, December 10, 2009, Regarding Sometime in 1974 and the Summer of 1980

I CAN'T HONESTLY SAY that Edith physically beat up on me often, but when she did, it was usually pretty brutal; and for things that I did not do. My most unforgettable are ones that happened when I was four and ten years old. The latter was a mopstick beatdown that I got in public one evening in the summer of 1980, on our very crowded block for an offense committed by my younger sister Nilda. She had sassed an adult—someone with whom I was unfamiliar—and people got our names confused often (my nickname, Nisey, was easy to confuse with Nilda), so I took the rap for that; with no allowance to convince Edith that it wasn't me.

The former whooping was the one that etched loneliness into my soul and made it easy for me to brush the mopstick beatdown under the rug.

Our family lived in a four-bedroom apartment on Bryant Avenue in The Bronx, during my fourth and fifth years. Two one-bedroom apartments had been combined to form one big one. The landlord had made an entryway connecting the living room of one apartment to the hallway of the other, and it was as if it had been a part of the original design. The kitchen and living room of the second apartment became bedrooms, and there were two full bathrooms and two front doors: one at the beginning of the second hallway, and one at the front of the other apartment, near the kitchen.

My sister Nilda, my aunt M and I shared a bedroom on the adjacent side. The view from our bedroom window, which was at the back of the building, was of tenements about a block away. It should have been of a tenement directly behind our building, but all that was there was a lot piled high with charred dirty mattresses, broken beer bottles, and enough debris for neighborhood kids to play tag and throw broken bits of brick at each other—remnants of the building that once stood there, which had suffered an all-destroying fire and was later demolished by the city. This type of view was commonplace in The South Bronx in the seventies; we—the children of the SB—thought nothing of romping around amongst discarded needles and beer cans, and adults didn't often interrupt us. Some would walk by: "You see dem kidz playin' in dat sh*t? They mamas should be 'shamed of theyself. That don' make no sense . . ."

My brother Harold and my uncle D shared the living-room-turned-bedroom, and my uncle B, his girlfriend Kay, and their daughter Tam shared the kitchen-turned-bedroom. Edith and Charlie slept in the bedroom on the other side of the apartment. There were a lot of us, but it all seemed to work.

MY YOUNGER SIBLINGS AND I spent a lot of time babysitting ourselves. There were always adults in the apartment, but we were usually playing in my bedroom by ourselves, unsupervised. On one particular afternoon, when this was the case, Kay was in her bedroom and my baby brother Jessie, who was almost two years old and running around diaper-less, took a crap in a plastic washbasin that our family had somehow acquired from a hospital stay.

We were playing, still, so no one noticed the load resting in the basin until Kay came into the bedroom and saw it. She wanted to know why I didn't do anything about it. I had no answers and she wouldn't let it die.

Uncle D came home and Kay went right to him with the news.

"Nisey let Jessie doodoo in the washbasin and she ain't tell nobody."

I don't recall much of what Uncle D said at first. He may have asked me "Why' you do that? Why you ain't tell nobody that Jessie doodoo'd in the basin?" But as I said, I don't recall. I do remember him having a sinister grin and a malicious look in his eyes when, as he was gathering together two long, thick leather belts, he told me to take all my clothes off.

He layered and doubled the belts and made an uninviting "Come hither" gesture with the pointer finger of his right hand . . .

I ran around. And I screamed. I think I actually slipped in little slicks of my own tears as I tried to escape the belts that seemed to land on every part of my body except my face. My running and screaming only excited Uncle D. His eyes were wild. He chased me; he swung harder. My pale yellow flesh wasn't much covering for the tiny muscles on my scrawny bones. I thought he was going to kill me. And I would have welcomed it if it freed me from the pain . . .

That whooping ended and Uncle D left. Kay told Edith when she got home, about the doodoo and the whooping. Edith had a thin, clear plastic belt with tiny flowers of many colors painted on it. This time, Kay, Aunt M, and Charlie were present; Harold was in the kitchen washing dishes. Again, I was made to take off my clothes. Naked-butt-whoopin's were a southern custom that migrated to the North; my mother's family was from Orangeburg, South Carolina.

Edith chased me throughout the apartment. I ran into the kitchen and collapsed at my brother Harold's feet as she continued to come down on me. Harold looked down at me, never ceasing his task. He quickly returned his compassion-filled-but-helpless eyes to the dishes. No need getting himself whooped trying to save me. Besides that, I was naked. Harold was my only friend. He wouldn't look upon me while I was exposed.

When part two was over, I redressed and went to my room to lie down. My body hurt everywhere and it was difficult to sleep. I wasn't even allowed to cry aloud. I had to hold it in until I could only just breathe; my only comfort was the tears that rained down my face that my floggers could not control. It was common practice in my family to spank a child and then tell them to shut up before they got something else to cry for. So if one wished to forego any additional thrashing, one had better suppress one's wail to an undetectable whimper. I unknowingly carried the tradition into my own parenting. Spanking is always my last resort; but I recall having shushed my children's cries after a good bottom lashing on occasion and hated myself for it.

I WENT TO MY BED AND TRIED TO LIE DOWN. I was so tired from running and screaming and crying . . . too tired to try to find a comfortable position . . . every part of me was covered in burning welts . . . the soreness of my back paled to my exhaustion as I lay my body on the worn springy mattress. I closed my eyes . . .

When I awoke, it was evening. Kay was gently nudging and whispering to me. When I opened my eyes, she was leaning over me, her face very close to mine, almost as if she was checking to see if I was still breathing.

"Come in the living room."

My last memory was of a butt-whoopin', so I could only imagine that that was what was waiting for me in the living room. But I didn't flinch, I didn't really even think much about it. As I reflect on it, I realize that there was either a built-in-something that protected me—kept me from breaking—or I was completely numb, already. I followed Kay as she led me by the hand to the living room.

Edith and Charlie were standing in the doorway of their bedroom which looked out into the living room where Aunt M, Harold, and Uncle B were waiting. Aunt M was sitting on the bed that was in the living room (We didn't have a couch; there were so many people living there that, I guess, beds were more important than furniture to sit on.).

Uncle B was standing in the middle of the floor with all the belts—the plastic flowery one, and the ones Uncle D had used—in his hands. What now? Why weren't the two beatings from earlier enough?

"Open your pajama top." Uncle B had a smile on his face, but he didn't look like he usually looked when one of us was getting whooped. This particular group of aunts and uncles considered it a spectator sport. No joke; we would be screamin' an' runnin' an' they would be laughin' till they were doubled over with tears in their eyes.

I unbuttoned my red and white checked top to reveal dark red raised half moons, arcs and bows, some of them thick, some thin, some overlapping and telling tale of the damage that the double and thin flowery belts had left behind.

"Who beat you? "
"Uncle D and Mommy."

Edith's head began to bobble.

"I ain't touch her."

I glanced over to where the voice had come from. She was standing in the doorway—lips full of lies—with a look on her face that I only stop short of calling stupid . . . idiotic . . . doofussy. I only knew my mother as one of the people I lived with; someone who dropped me off with whomever was convenient, who never talked to me unless I was in the way, never hugged me, never ever told me she loved me. So at this moment, while she was chillin' in the doorway of her bedroom with her arms crossed, telling that lie with no alibi (and not one of the people who had witnessed her hitting me willing to expose her), I knew one thing for certain: I did not like her and I wanted to get away from her forever.

"Well, somebody beat her. "
"Well, it wasn't me." She had said it again. I think her having repeated the lie hurt more than the two beatings I had endured.

Uncle D came in while Uncle B was still examining my bruises. He asked him the same question he had asked Edith.

"I didn't touch her!"

Uncle D repeated this over and over as he jumped up and down, wild-eyed, huffing and puffing in feigned disbelief and anger.

I could do nothing with what I was hearing. If not for the bruises that I would see every time I undressed for the next several months, I would have thought that I had dreamt the whole thing.

This was when I learned for sure that Edith couldn't be trusted. I already knew Uncle D couldn't; he had tried several weeks earlier to have sex with me. He had me pinned down on his bed with my legs crushed against my chest, applying to his member every lubricant that he could get his hands on, trying at first desperately and then angrily (I was screaming and begging him to stop and it was ticking him off) to penetrate me, but he gave up after several tries. He was so angry; I was surprised he didn't kill me. Replaying this in my mental is so surreal; for years, whenever I told this story I almost disassociated. But I can't do that anymore.

It's real and live to me; I am ten times the age I was when it occurred and I only took it seriously while it was happening; but I look at it now and realize how Uncle D could have torn my insides to shreds; how he could have literally killed me with his penis; surely my cervix and my uterus were all one tiny little lump taking up a small space somewhere very near to the opening of my little vagina; there's no way that the monstrosity between his legs would not have cut through my bladder and whatever organs were in line with it; he would have gutted me; I can only imagine what the obituary (if they bothered to write one)—the epitaph on my tombstone (if they had bothered to buy one)—would have read; what would they have said at the funeral? What would have happened to Uncle D? Back then, these things were kept secret.

They would probably have buried me in that vacant lot—the backdrop of my very life. But there was an angel between Uncle D's phallus and my womb. What a place for an angel to have to work . . .

Daddy

Journal, Fall 2008; Regarding December 3, 1983

> *"In a real dark night of the soul, it is always three o'clock in the morning, day after day."*
>
> —F. Scott Fitzgerald

NEXT TO MY BROTHER HAROLD, my grandfather was my best friend in the whole world. We called him Daddy. He wouldn't let us prefix it with "Grand" because he said it made him feel old. And he was serious about that. Daddy always treated me extra special. His birthday was on Christmas and mine is December 22.

He lived on 135th Street and Broadway, in Harlem. I used to take the bus or the train there from The Bronx on my own; had been doing so since I was eight years old. I remember cashing in my tokens on each trip (at the time, they cost fifty cents) and walking onto the crosstown bus, or under the subway turnstile, for free. No one ever stopped me, or even questioned my traveling solo so young.

Daddy was a meanie, but I didn't care. I could run to him whenever Edith got on my nerves and he would console me and blast her. He was a great chef, baker, electrician, carpenter. He made his own devices—like a universal remote that controlled the television and the stereo system—way before people even had remote controls for their televisions alone. He made lamps and beds and desks and all kinds of stuff. But my favorite of all things were his strawberry cheesecake and his fudge. The man was a master of everything he did.

I loved going to Daddy's house around Christmas time. I knew I could always count on him to make that time special for me.

It was December 3, 1982. It was a Friday. I had just bought a ten-pack of five-stick packs of Doublemint gum (a total of 50 pieces). I was going to give them out on my birthday to all my friends at school, like a friend of mine had done earlier that year. I was sitting in the living room in Daddy's leather lounge chair. I was opening the gum, eating much of it, and counting it out so I could attach ribbons that I would pin to my friends in nineteen days. The gum never made it out of the living room. I had a thing for Doublemint; I should have known better. Daddy had a thing for sweets, too.

"Come here, Denise."[7]

There was an enclave in the center of the apartment, to the left of the living room past the kitchen, between all the bedrooms and bathrooms. It was where the ironing board and other essentials were kept. He was ironing.

"You didn't even kiss me hello when you came in."

I tiptoed and pecked him on his cheek.

"You're a big girl, now. You know how to kiss better than that."

He bent down and put his mouth to mine. His tongue. I was wearing that stripy turtleneck again, the one with the run in it. It was too small for me. By now, my breasts were beyond puberty. He had a hand on them. He was rubbing. (To this day, I can't stand being touched that way through my clothes. Until now, I didn't know the reason why.)

I opened my eyes and saw that his were closed. I closed mine again. I don't know if I kissed back.

I usually do what they want.

---

[7] My birth name was Denise. My name changed to QuYahni in 1995.

My insides turn to vomit, but I always recover quickly. This time, though, I began to die. There was this incessant screaming inside my head.

No-no-no-no-no-no-no!

There was a brokenness that kept happening over and over again. And the pieces—of my heart, my esteem, my hope—fell never-ending with each ineffable cry. Tearless—me wanted to fall to the floor and bawl and scratch at the linoleum until there was blood, until I felt nothing, until I slipped into the place I always go. On this night, I didn't make it there.

The others—I saw them coming; I knew what they would bring and I accepted it because it had become my life. I did not see Daddy; not in this way. I needed him not to be that way. Whatever was left of me—the tiny flicker that made me believe that some part of my childhood would be left unmarred—slipped away. As it floated away in slow motion, reaching out to me and saying "good-bye" all at once, I knew I was not going to trust anymore. And, for a long time, I would not be trusted. I disappeared; the hope of me; the belief that there was more to me; better in me; it retreated to a place that was deep, flooded, murky, and formless.

A key was in the lock and a knob was turning. Minnie and Alvin were home[8]. They couldn't see us from where they were.

Daddy pulled away. I ran to the bathroom to wash my face, my mouth, my tongue. Water was useless to me. I looked in the mirror. I'm not sure who was there. My refuge was gone.

---

[8] Minnie was common-law wife and Alvin was the youngest of the three children Daddy had outside of his marriage to my maternal grandmother.

Some Robert, Some Jessie

Journal Entry, July 2009; Regarding Wednesday, March 10, 1982

I LEFT SCHOOL A LITTLE EARLY and met Robert on East Tremont and Bathgate Avenue in The Bronx. We stopped at a corner diner and he bought me a tuna sub and 7-Up. I was twelve years old. I had not allowed him the adventure he'd been asking, but I could still get him to give me a couple of bucks here and there. It was never more than four dollars, but it was enough for what I needed, when I needed it. He was still trying to convince me that his request was innocuous, that it was something commonplace and normal. I remember the first time he suggested it two years prior.

Robert lived in a room on the ground floor of a Bronx rooming house on Morris Avenue, near Burnside Avenue. He had false teeth and a pacemaker that stuck out of his chest like a pack of cigarettes in a shirt pocket, and he chewed peach snuff that he spit into an old coffee can that he kept nearby. He was the godfather of a friend, or at least, that's what she called him. She introduced us sometime around spring 1980. She took me to visit him and he gave us money. He was real touchy-feely, but I was used to men like that. He told me I could come by at anytime. So I did. A lot.

One day, while another child and I were visiting, he called me to a vacant room in the back. There was a bed and dresser with a mirror in there. He leaned his backside against the dresser and motioned me to his arms, between his legs. He held me close. He wanted to talk about me in the night on a roof with a stranger once upon a few-months-before. I didn't. I fell silent. My body went stiff.

"What did he do to you?"

(No words from me; couldn't respond.)

"I can teach you about sex. Anytime you want to know about sex, you come to me. Okay?"

I nodded my head in affirmation. I didn't want to, I just didn't know how to respond. I knew I had to make sure I was never alone with him again. I would still come to visit because he gave me money and candy, but I had to make sure there was always another kid around.

A bunch of kids from the block—at least ten of us—spent the night at his place once. When I went to sleep on the floor, I was surrounded by various warm bodies about my size. I slept like a rock. When I woke up the next morning, my hand was resting in a thick gooey substance. I had knocked over Robert's spit can. I was horrified, but my disgust quickly turned to fear when I noticed that a little baby who was asleep on the bed and I were the only ones left in his room. Robert was sitting on the bed next to the baby.

"I think I knocked over your can. I'm sorry. "
"It's okay. I'll clean it up. Go, take a shower and I'll come and dry you off. "
"I don't need help. I know how to dry myself." (. . . more words in my head that never made it to my lips.)

I took a shower. I tried to take a really long time. I dried myself off and I waited. I waited because he had taken my clothes, so I would have to come out naked, or in a towel. There was nowhere else to go and there was no lock on the bathroom door. He walked in and saw me with the towel around myself.

"Why didn't you call me? Here, let me dry you off . . ."

I was completely dry already, so there was no need. He knew this but he toweled me anyway. And lotioned me. And dressed me. But even this wasn't enough to keep me away. I always needed money.

So nearly two years later, on this March 10 afternoon while we waited in the diner for my tuna sandwich, he asked me, again, about his proposition.

"Have you thought about what I asked you? Are you going to try it? "
"Try what? "
"You know what. We talked about this before."

I really don't remember what my answer was. I was so sassy when I addressed him. I actually got all-up-in his face in public and talked to him like he was my age. Like he was my man.

"You said you was gonna give me some money. When you gonna gimme my money? Why 'you keep askin' me to let you teach me about sex, don't you know how old I am?" (Now, this, I actually said.)

I tried to string him along and get what I wanted without giving him what he wanted. But it was wearing thin. He was getting tired of asking. I was about to lose my stream of income. He only gave me pocket change as it was. He never gave me the big stuff—the tens and twenties—that I really needed.

And he never actually said he wanted to do me. He never used the actual words. He was pretty smart for a dummy. Why did he think that a girl who had already been molested actually wanted to be? And by a fifty-two-year-old man? He walked me to the #40 bus stop, told me to stop playing games, and went about his business.

That would be the last time I would leave his presence without submitting to his request. As the bus turned the corner from University Avenue onto Burnside Avenue, I saw police activity in front of PS 26BX. Mine was the next stop—Burnside and Hennessy Place. I got off, crossed the street, went into our building, number 1900, on the corner. We lived in one of those tenement buildings with a left and right wing. My family lived on the right, on the first floor. A neighbor, Michelle, who lived on the left, on one of the upper floors (I believe it was the third), was walking ahead of me, escorted by two police officers. She was crying and they were consoling her. As I entered the building behind them, she looked back, saw my face and cried even harder. The officers stopped and comforted her;

I walked past them. I went inside our first floor apartment, said hello to Edith. She was in the kitchen. Aunt M was in the bathtub with her toddler Ava. I stood in the open doorway of the bathroom and talked to her while I ate my tuna sub. The doorbell rang.

Voices that I didn't recognize were coming from the living room. I turned my attention to them and saw the two officers that had been with our neighbor only a few minutes before. I looked at Edith . . .

"Mommy, what happened . . ." She was still looking at the officers. She appeared not to hear my query . . .

"Jessie got hit by a bus?" Edith looked confused. "No. Jessie's in school. Not my Jessie . . ."

MY VISION BLURRED. My tuna sub—what was left in my hand and the lump that I had just bitten off that sat in my open mouth—fell to the floor. I screamed. My feet left the ground and met the ground, left the ground and met the ground in a raging and continuous disbelieving stomp as I tried to understand what I had just heard. Aunt M was climbing out of the tub, snatching up Ava, as the officers stepped into the bathroom doorway. She didn't seem to remember that she was naked. The officers tried to calm us. Edith kept repeating " . . . not my Jessie, Jessie's in school . . ." She blinked repeatedly, her head dipped and rocked like a bobble head doll (she had a nervous condition; her siblings said it was from an accident she had as a teenager; she had to bobble her head to focus her eyes; they didn't work well) . . . she watched Aunt M and me scream . . .

I was wearing Jessie's lilac short-sleeved button-down shirt that day; it was a boys' shirt, but it matched exactly my girls' dress pants of the same color. I had been talking about him to my best schoolmates at lunch. I never talked about my younger siblings. It just wasn't like that with us. We couldn't stand each other—all we ever did was fight. Tears enveloped me as I remembered the conversation he and I had on the Monday afternoon before. It was the day that I heard on the radio for the first time that John Belushi had died[9].

---

9   John Belushi died on March 5, 1982. I heard about it on the radio on Monday, March 8,1982. (I just realized that he and Jessie shared initials, too:

Jessie had come home from school early. He had peed in his pants and asked to borrow a pair of mine. There was fear in his eyes—I know he thought of the beating that would come if Mommy or Charlie found out.[10] A playful slap to his butt was my signal to him to hurry and wash while the coast was clear. I gave him my green corduroys.[11] He smiled at me. I was warm inside; happy to keep his secret. This was a new feeling for me. It was the revelation of love.

ALL THROUGH THE RATTLING and jerking of my body, as the tears pushed and consumed and I gave birth in raw, dry, burning labor to the reality that my baby brother was dead, all the love I never knew I had and never showed him—all the trouble our lives had been—ate holes into me and pushed their way into my eye sockets and bled wet salt all over my tortured face, all over my hands that clutched at my tortured face, all over my Coke-bottle-bottomed glasses, all over Jessie's lilac shirt.

It was soon cleared up—Jessie had not been hit by a bus—he had hitched a ride on the outside of the back door of one of the new oblong MTA buses that had nothing to hold onto.[12] His friends were behind him, on the back of a delivery truck. They made it off alive with a visual branded into their memories that I'm sure they could have done without.

Jessie died doing something that was normal for him . . . being defiant . . . taking chances . . . finding joy and adventure in the forbidden because his only male role models were abusive drug addicts whom he

---

J.B. for Jessie Bell.)

[10] Charlie used to beat Jessie for the most menial of offenses; anything from not combing his hair to taking too long to walk past the television.

[11] Edith (Mommy) sometimes bought me boys' pants. Jessie and I shared

[12] These GMC RTS-II Coach buses were introduced in NYC ca. 1981; the GM buses that preceded them had windows that were easy to open; many a wayward child/teen hitched a ride on the side of those buses by hanging from the window by the arm. The GMC RTS-II's windows that opened upwards and outwards from the inside; there was no way to hold on unless you started from inside the bus and climbed out the window.

watched defile his mother and take food out of his mouth. He probably had a smile on his face . . . even while airborne . . .

> I needed another moment.
> The time I spent cajoling a tuna sub and two dollars from a pedophile,
> I needed that back.
> It had only been minutes before Jessie daredevil-tripped the side of the bus,
> before it turned the corner and threw him to the ground,
> before it destroyed the right side of his cocoa face,
> his nine-year-old brains,
> one beautiful brown eye.
> They all kissed the concrete hard and like Jesus on his cross-journey
> he was barely identifiable,
> only a mother would know him.
> Death did not linger,
> it had mercy and took him quick,
> and with him went any chance of a real
> brother-sister-,
> Jessie-Nisey-[13],
> love.

IT WAS NOT JESSIE IN THE COFFIN. It couldn't have been. His face had been reconstructed on the right side. The doctors said that, had he lived, he'd have lost his right eye. His skin was darker, his head was bigger—boxy and square-like—and his beauty was hidden. He didn't look sad or like he'd been in any pain at all. He appeared happy, almost smiling. I still wanted to believe it wasn't him, but his mouth was a dead giveaway. It was still ringed with discoloration from the chapped lips he'd had that past winter. I had teased him about it, told him it made him look like he had a mustache. I never told him that I thought it was cute.

---

[13] Nisey was my childhood nickname.

"Yeah, it's definitely him," my mind accepted, finally. I stood at the casket in my borrowed white frills and pressed curls and tried to cry. The tears that had not denied me for days seemed to have run dry. There would be more in the weeks to come, but I couldn't find them just then, when I needed them most, when I knelt before Jessie and studied his new, darkened face.

Days became months and, even though I knew better, I continued to wrestle with the idea that Jessie wasn't really dead. I wasn't crazy; I just held onto the hope that it had been a mistake. That it was someone else's baby brother buried beneath the bitter earth and that Jessie had finally gotten away from us, from this hyper-dysfunction, from this life as it was for us. I was fine visiting that unreality until he invaded my sleep one night when I was seventeen.

HE WAS OLDER in this dream—about fourteen—the age he would have been had he not died. He was muscular. He had on his strong-man-face; not the fake one that was necessary to navigate his childhood; but a real confidence . . . strength . . . peace. His hands rested on his hips, his thumbs in his front pockets. He was smiling. I wasn't. I was mad at him.

"Why did you do that, Jessie? Why did you make us think that you were dead for all these years?"

He didn't answer. He lowered his eyes to the floor and offered a familiar snicker; his I-don't-really-know-why-and-I-don't-care snicker; the one that he had used to hurt those who would have crushed him. Only, it wasn't debasing. He simply had nothing to care about anymore. I didn't know I missed his laughter.

I cried myself awake, abruptly sitting up in my bed in the room I shared with my cousins DeVonni and Keisha.[14] They had not yet known death, but they knew pain. They stayed up with me until I returned to sleep.

---

[14] When I was seventeen, due to some pretty heavy stuff that went down at Edith's apartment (which I'm sure, by now, you can imagine), BCW (Bureau of Child Welfare), now known as ACS (Agency for Child Services), deemed our house unfit for the inhabitance of children, so I became a foster child while I was visiting my Aunt Delores and her three children, Robert, DeVonni and

Everywhere I Go

Journal Entry, Thursday, January 5, 2006; Regarding Summer 1985

I RAN INTO JOUNIE during the summer of 1985. I hadn't seen him since I was twelve years old, at least. I had very few good memories of him; I don't think I had any at all. He was a part of my Run-Catch-and-Kiss phase. One of my worst memories of him, though, was shortly after that night on the purple rooftop. He had just come back from a corner store with a drink in his hand. I was on the steps of the tenement that we both lived in, 1900 Hennessy Place.[15] He stopped directly below me and opened his drink, took a sip.

"Whew! This soda tastes like piss!"
"Giggle . . . silly, how could you know what piss tastes like?"
"I don't . . . but I know you do . . ."

My heart fell as the words left his mouth; it pretty much fell as my query left mine because I knew I had set myself up. And then, five years later . . . I didn't see this encounter coming . . . this encounter at the pizza shop near Fordham Road . . .

    Keisha. They let me stay and I had been living there for about four months when I had this dream.

[15] My family lived in many different residences in The Bronx, New York. Unless otherwise indicated, most every street name I mention is in The Bronx.

It was early evening. It was summer. It was my first year wearing contact lenses. The solution irritated my eyes. I had gotten some drops from the optician to remedy it, but they hadn't yet taken effect. My eyes were bloodshot when Jounie walked into the pizza shop where my best friend, her boyfriend, my boyfriend (his cousin), and I were waiting for our food.

Jounie, my boyfriend, his cousin—they all seemed to know each other. They gave each other pound while Jounie smirked at me. His eyes were mocking, but I told myself he was trying to figure out if he recognized me from somewhere.

"Hi, Jounie. It's me, Nisey—Edith's daughter, I used to wear glasses, remember?"

Apprehension gripped my chest. I was self-conscious . . . my eyes must have looked like hell. I had hoped that the absence of the thick glasses would save me from the usual derision.

"Yeah, I know who you are. What the eff happened to your eyes?"

Laughter—roaring laughter—from everyone that was with me. Jounie continued to smirk at me. His eyes lit up; his affront had scored. I melted . . .

"I know . . . my contact lenses . . . the solution irritated my eyes . . ."

Jounie continued to make jokes. They continued to laugh. I pretended to laugh too. The knot in the pit of my stomach grew; I could swear I was distended. The taunting look in his eyes and the smirk on his face brought reminiscence that I never seemed to have time to recover from. It was always coming. And it was so easy for him; it was so easy for them, even the ones that should have loved me at least a little bit.

All the prettying up I thought I had done; all the getting-rid-of-the-thick-glasses; all the changing of my hair; none of it meant anything. Instantly, I became bummy four-eyed Denise all over again. Right then, every molester I had ever known had his hands in me. Nothing on the outside would change what was already implanted. This was going to take far more than I would get at that time.

It seemed like forever before our pizza was ready, before I got away from Jounie. But I carried it with me. It's been twenty-three years. Nothing so ugly should stay inside of anyone so long.

The Burning

Journal Entry, July 2009; Regarding November 25-December 18, 1985

I WAS SO TIRED WHEN I GOT HOME that afternoon. Edith was there. Our lights were out again. She hadn't paid the ConEd bill. It was late fall and it was after 5:00 p.m., so it was dark and I had to feel my way around the small, junky one-bedroom apartment that was shared by Edith, Charlie, Nilda, and me (and many long-term visitors, on occasion).

I ran my free hand along the wall that led to the bedroom I lived in with Nilda and held onto my book-bag with the other. The ironing board was open and took up much of the space in front of my bed, which was right by our bedroom door. I dropped my book-bag and felt around on the ironing board for the candle and the matches that I used to light it the night before. I lit the candle and, without undressing, threw myself down on the bed, surrounded by a huge fire hazard of strewn clothes, papers, whatnot.

I closed my eyes and listened to the pulsing of my vagina. It was vibrating through my body. Something wasn't right. I searched my head for all the information I had soaked up from the giant medical book Edith got from one of those clearing-house offers. I wanted this thing that I knew I had that wasn't gonna just disappear to be a urinary tract infection. I let that hope lull me to sleep as my thoughts tossed between it and the reason I was contemplating any condition in the first place . . .

It was itching... burning... itch-burning. And it was taking too long. We had been at it for more than three hours. I began glancing periodically at the digital clock radio at the side of the bed after about an hour, I think. After about an hour and a half and several changes in position, I began to stare at the clock, hoping it would explode; anything to make him stop.

I had heard of longevity, but this just made no sense. I wasn't all that experienced. Before Corwin, I had had three intentional penetrations and one forced. None of them lasted more than a few minutes. But Corwin was not letting up.

Was he trying to impress me? He surely didn't need to. I just wanted to experience this with him and know that he would still respect me afterward. But what was he doing?

It was over at about four o'clock. We had planned this meeting. Corwin had made arrangements to use the place his brother rented in a rooming house. We cut school and took the train to a Northeast Bronx brownstone not far from the ell. If I remember correctly, it was the number two or five train.

I was so excited to be with Corwin. Beautiful brown skin, Gherri Curl with a D.A. haircut, the latest fashions, athletic. He was one of the pretty boys and I was amazed that he wanted me. Me and my thick glasses. Sleeping with him would be an honor.

We had been dating for about a month before he brought it up. I thought that was so noble. He waited for me, only kissed me, never touched me inappropriately. So perfect.

While we were at his brother's, while what started out as sweet and beautiful began to feel like cruel and unusual punishment, I tried to step outside my own body and ride it out until he was done. Yet three hours later, after we had abandoned the bedroom, he made one more attempt in the shower. Body beleaguered, mind searching but too exhausted to question, I further loaned myself to his endeavor. But it was ephemeral; my heart genuflected and silently thanked God for the end to my own personal porn horror movie.

We dressed and left. A few hugs and gentle kisses and we parted ways at the ell; he had to go uptown, I had to go down. I went home to a dark apartment.

. . . I AWOKE TO A SOFT TOUCH. I looked up and, in the flickering candlelight I saw Cisco, Charlie's Puerto Rican friend. He was sitting at the foot of my bed, his hand resting on my thigh. I bolted upright and adjusted my glasses. Nope, not a dream.

"Excuse me, please."

He moved out of my way as I scooted to my feet. I went looking for Edith, who had been there when I fell asleep.

"Where's my mother? "
"She left. She let me in and she went downstairs."

He followed me about the tiny apartment as I went from room to room, looking for any one of the people that I lived with. Cisco was right. Edith really did leave me alone with him.

He was babbling about some money Edith had asked for to pay the ConEd bill.

"I don't know if I'm really gonna give it her. I was thinkin' of givin' it to you, jus' in case you need some clothes for school. What'choo think I should do? "
"You should jus' give it to my mother. "
"You sure? You don't need nothin'? Can I buy you some clothes? Give you some money for yo' pockets? "
"No, I don't need anything. "
"You sure? "
"Yeah, I'm sure. "
"Okay, well you let me know if you ever need anything . . ."

Even the weak fluttering glow couldn't mask the lust in his eyes. My raw and irritated young womanhood was now joined by crawling skin and heebie-jeebies. If he knew of the bushfire that was ablaze down there he would probably change his mind. Probably.

I was a little teed off, but not surprised that Edith had left me sleeping alone in a dark apartment with a horny pedophile, and I was too annoyed by the itching to really care about this man and his motives. But I also knew he wasn't too far from jumping me. *Lord, if he tries anything, he dies tonight.* I decided that getting out of their fast was the best way to avoid having a reason to explain a man sprawled out somewhere in our apartment with his penis ripped off.

I grabbed my coat and told Cisco that I was going out to look for my mom; his cue to get the hell out. As we descended the five flights of stairs, Cisco followed closely behind me and rambled on about how much he wanted to take care of me, until we both saw Edith outside standing on our tenement steps. The two of them talked briefly, he gave her the money, threw one last *I-wanna-get-in-your-drawers* smile my way, and went about his business. I didn't even bother to ask Edith why she left. I went back upstairs. I had to pee. I hadn't been to the bathroom since before Corwin and I cut school.

IT WAS AN INTERESTING FEELING. Not quite burning, but definitely uncomfortable. I decided to go look up some stuff in the medical book one more time, just to see.

I couldn't blame what I saw on the dimness of candlelight flicker. It wasn't a UTI. It wasn't trichomonas, chlamydia, or any other mild nuisance. It wasn't AIDS, herpes, or syphilis, thank God. But it was definitely a force to be reckoned with.

It was thanksgiving week and we only had school Monday through Wednesday. Corwin asked me to come see him on Wednesday night. I took the long train ride to The Northeast Bronx, met him in his living room (he barely let me in his house—I had to stand in the entryway. There was a rift between his aunt and him; she was who he lived with). We went into their backyard and climbed into the backseat of an old wheel-less car. We had sex, again.

Initially, the friction was scratching the itch so I didn't mind so much. But then, it began to burn. I didn't say anything. And, again, it was taking too long.

Corwin walked me to the train and I braved the long, late night ride to 174th and Jerome Avenue, the dark lonely walk from there to our apartment on Weeks Avenue; all the while thinking and praying that I didn't catch something that I couldn't get rid of, still content in my relationship with Corwin, ignoring the obvious and clinging to my hope for a silver lining.

I HAD SUDDENLY LOST my appetite and hadn't eaten since the night I went to see Corwin. I was feeling a little weird when Edith took me shopping for a winter coat the day after Thanksgiving. We had already paid for my coat and were standing in line at Alexander's on Fordham Road with some other merchandise when I began to feel dizzy.

"Mommy . . . I can't stand up . . ."

Edith was standing in front of me. I fell forward in slow motion and my body leaned against hers. Everything in front of my eyes was spotty and I couldn't hold myself up. Edith threw the stuff down on the counter and dragged me out to the street as she cussed me for messin' up her plans. We caught a taxi home, climbed the five flights to the apartment with me clinging to her and slowing her down. I threw myself on the bed and drifted off.

"She' fakin'—ain't nuffin' wrong wit' huh."

My mother's sister, Aunt M, had spent the night with us for Thanksgiving. She never thought any of us were ever sick. She told me to go get some food, but I didn't move.

"Oh, hell no! She ain't eatin'?! Now I know somethin's wrong! Gimme a thermometer . . ."

I had a temperature of 104 degrees. Edith and I took a taxi three blocks to Bronx Lebanon Hospital. There was a short wait in the emergency room. The doctor's painful speculum invasion told no lies. He whispered to the nurse, but I heard him clearly. I was still hoping, though.

The doctors sent us home and told us they would call with the test results. It wasn't long before the message came that I needed to return and be admitted to the hospital.

THAT WAS DECEMBER 1, 1985. The conflagration in my young but far-too-experienced vagina was PID (pelvic inflammatory disease), a form of gonorrhea. I was strapped to a pole with IV pumping antibiotics that made me pee fire for the first five days. Then there was a vaginal suppository to get rid of the Ghost-Buster-slime discharge. Ten lonely days of hospitalization led to eighteen because the PID had caused a cyst to develop on one of my ovaries. I got butt shots every six hours during those extra eight days. The nurse that gave me my first shot, and my evening and overnight shots, was a curmudgeon. She yelled at me with thick Jamaican accent because I had misunderstood—I thought that the shots were to be administered in my arm like vaccinations.

"You knew dis wuz comin'! Dey tol' you you wuz gettin' it in deh hip! Lay down an' turn over on yah side!"

She practically threw me down and stabbed me in the butt. I cried myself to sleep that first night. My butt didn't hurt; I was just embarrassed. I felt violated. And I wanted to punch that old lady in her face.

CORWIN HAD ONLY CALLED ME ONCE while I was in the hospital, and only came to see me twice—each time with only fifteen minutes left before visiting hours were over. I knew exactly how long the visits were because I watched the clock every day, waiting for him to show up. During the last visit, he asked me for money. I would have given him anything. I missed him so much.

Corwin said that the doctor gave him one shot in the butt and had him taking pills. We used our fifteen-minute visit to talk about the new developments in his life. He had figured out who he had gotten the disease from. A disagreement with his aunt got him kicked out. He was living at Covenant House, somewhere in Manhattan. He kissed me, hugged me like he loved me, took the money and left.

By the time I got out of the hospital, school was out for Christmas break. My closest schoolmate, Michelle, was good friends with Corwin; at least until after she had spoken with him about what happened. She called me to break the news.

"Denise, Corwin knew he had a disease all along. "
"What? "
"He knew he had a disease *before* he had sex with you! "

"What?" I wasn't hard of hearing and there was nothing wrong with the phone. What she was saying just didn't make sense.

"Yes, he did, Denise. I just got off the phone with him. He said he knew all along. "

"Well, that explains a lot . . ."

So Corwin hadn't "figured out" who he had gotten the disease from. He knew he was combustible before he lit into me. That's why he was taking so long when we were making love. He had to hold his ejaculation because it burned his urethra. Either that or he thought I wouldn't catch it if he didn't release. But why on earth would he do that? Why would he do that when he knew there was something wrong with him; something that could hurt me, too?

I rehearsed everything; the entire eighteen days; the afternoon of endless penetration; the memories overtook me. I was boiling mad. Suddenly, as it should have when I saw him walk through the door at Bronx Lebanon Hospital, it mattered to me that he only came to see me twice and only spent fifteen minutes with me each time, talking about himself; asking me for money and leaving like it was nothing. I sat contrasting his one shot and bottle of pills to my month of December in the hospital being a test-dummy for probing, fumbling interns, enduring round-the-clock butt shots, merciless antibiotics, heartless nurses and loneliness. I seethed; I flashed back to the hours he spent burning that disease into my flesh; the audacity he had to summon me two nights later to do it again in the backseat of a filthy old car out in the November cold; how he further ground his disease into me and didn't even take me home. I was even angrier that I had availed myself to it all.

I sent the breakup message to Corwin through Michelle. Several months later he approached me during my practice for a school talent show. He apologized for what he had done and asked me if I would be with him again.

"Corwin, I love you. I really do. But you hurt me. You didn't think about me at all. I spent a lot of time trying to figure out why someone would do what you did, and I still don't know why. I can't be with you again."

I said some more stuff and sat emotionless as tears fell from his eyes. He left. And I went on searching for love.

I CAUGHT MY SECOND STD from a guy named Brian when I was seventeen.

This one was sneaky; it had been hiding in my body for about four months before it showed itself. No five-alarm fire like the gift Corwin gave me. My doctor (Dr. Johnson, she treated me as if I were her own; she was a clinic doctor who didn't know [or didn't care] about the unwritten rule that did not allow for having genuine feelings for one's ghetto patients; it broke her heart to tell me I had been burnt yet again; I could see it in her eyes), she was real gentle with me (I was bent over getting a giant butt shot in addition to having to swallow sixteen pills in one sitting), but she also wanted me to understand how important it was to protect myself. Yet I never did.

I didn't even think about it. Even after doing extensive research on AIDS for a school presentation. Even after PID, which could have rendered me sterile. I don't think I did it on purpose; I wasn't trying to die. I just didn't think beyond the need to be held, accepted, loved. There never seemed to be any time to think. When one relationship ended, one was on the way. It was almost as if someone was watching and waiting and sending the badness as soon as I was out of one horrible episode. After a while, the relationships began to bump into each other. It was rare that I was faithful to one man; I had simultaneous lovers, some who knew of the others' existence, others who thought they were the only ones, some in love with me, most just out for the drama I brought, games I played. I didn't know it then, but all I really wanted was one person's genuine affirmation. And all along there was Someone Who I only acknowledged when I recited "Now I lay me down to sleep" and "God is great and God is good" or when I was in a whole lotta trouble. Until He became more to me than a kiddy prayer, my life would be a sad and haunting reprise.

I Knew It Was Time to Go

Journal Entry, November 2008; Regarding October 1986-November 1992)

"YOU LOOK GOOD IN THE DARK. "
"Ha-ha-ha-ha-ha-ha . . . gee, thanks. "
"How do I look?"
I couldn't answer. Something was different.
"Do I look scary? "
"Yeah . . ."

My heart was not cooperating with me. It was punching its way through my chest. What in hell was wrong with me? What in hell was wrong with *him?* His face changed. Or maybe it was always this way and I was seeing for the first time.

I heard him say before that he needed to choose. Once, only once did he look distressed, like he didn't know what to do.

"I have a path to take, but I have to decide if I'm going to choose my father's way, or the other way."

Your father? Who's your father? These were only mind-questions. He did all the asking. I just listened and figured things out for myself.

"My father's way is not a good way, but I have to choose . . ."

He said some more stuff that made it pretty clear. It was a choice between heaven or hell; and not just you and me trying to decide whether or not we were gonna start going to church or if, when we got there, we were gonna go up to the altar. He was in a quandary, like, "hmmm, demon or angel, which one do I wanna be?"

Even with no real idea of spiritual things, I knew what he was talking about. He was on some Satanism crap. Other than the uncomfortable and unsanitary things he required of me during intercourse, and the strange way he dressed, Pretty Ricky seemed "normal." There were no scary rituals, no blood sacrifices, no upside down crosses or anything like that. Maybe it was too soon for all that. Maybe he had to rope me in before he laid the heavy stuff on me.

I don't know. But before this night, I didn't care. I needed to be oblivious. It had to be just Pretty and me; him loving me in his special way; him making me feel like he needed me. Like, one time, in the elevator. He was making me leave again. He had something important to do.

"I haven't been with anyone since I've been with you—I swear. I love you."

I believed him. He kept saying it.

"I love you."

His smile was so beautiful. And he was looking *into* me. He held my chin in his hand and stuffed money into mine as the elevator doors closed between us with me inside, him standing in the hallway outside of his apartment, half-naked.

"I swear, it's only been you."

His kiss was soft and crossed with love and lasciviousness. If there could be such a thing.

I WAS ONLY ALLOWED to see Pretty when he called. But that wasn't enough for me.

I would call and hang up when I heard his voice. I would wait thirty minutes and I would walk the four blocks to his apartment. He didn't even know I had his number. I got it by accident, sorta.

I was almost asleep one night when I stayed with him, and I overheard him give his number to another girl on the phone. She was to be my wake-up call for school the following morning. I memorized the number before I closed my eyes that night. I had to; I never knew when I would see him again.

This night started just that way. He hadn't called in a while and I missed him. It was about two o'clock in the morning. I knew he would be home and my call-hang-up method confirmed it. But he wasn't answering the buzzer. I knew he was there; I had heard his voice on the phone only minutes before. I had been there for twenty minutes. I buzzed one last time and left the building. I would just go home and call again. And I would keep coming back until he let me in.

"Psst! Priscilla!" (I don't know why he called me that. He called all of us—all of his women—that.) I looked up. His pretty face was in the window looking down at me. Was I skipping? I hope I wasn't skipping. I got off the elevator and ran right into him. He grabbed me by the neck and snatched me into the apartment. His pupils were darker than usual.

"What the eff is wrong with you?"
"Nothing. "
"Then why the eff were you ringing the bell like that? "
"I don't know. "
"Why do you think I didn't answer the door? "
"Maybe you didn't want anyone to know you were here. "
"Right. So what the eff is wrong with you? Do you think I want you to be crazy over me? I was about to come down with the eff-in gun! Then what? "
"I'm sorry."

(He spewed lots of words that I don't remember; at least five minutes of yellin' an' cussin')

"Don't you ever do anything like that again, you hear me? "
"Yes. "

"So . . ." his face softened, I thought, and his lips turned up into a creepy smile " . . . how ya doin'? "

"Fine."

JUST LIKE THAT, the warped and screaming Pretty morphed into the one I had come to know. He began talking about himself. He always did and he didn't really ask much about me. Unless it was nasty . . .

"Would you ever have sex with a girl? "
"No. "
"Why not? "
"Because it's nasty. "
"No it's not. It's the same thing."

He always thought I was there for the sex. They all did. Why? I never, ever had an orgasm; they never tried to please me; what made them think they were so good?

So tonight, like any other night, he talked; about all the songs he wrote (and he sang them to me—words cannot express the horror); all the women he slept with (who now belong to him); all the STDs he'd contracted (except HIV and herpes); something about a mother-daughter or niece-aunt affair (a grown woman and teenage girl competing over a seventeen-year-old?); the tough, street girls (even they belonged to him); how he could have any of my friends; my sister; whoever he wanted; how he would never do for me the things he had me do for him with my mouth . . .

That might have been what he was talking about. I couldn't really hear him anymore. He had never been angry with me before and I had been careful to keep it that way. I had heard his anger once while he was on the phone with another girl. He took everything he knew about her and spat it at her; ripped her to shreds and then put the receiver to my lips so she could listen to my faux moans while his body made assault against my tender teenage cervix.

I didn't want to know such anger. I wanted to be his perfect princess. He always had such nice things to say about me . . .

"You're so giving . . . you really can sing . . . I like these (my breasts)."

He seemed to really want me around. Only me. We were everything. Even if it was strange and secret and dirty and just sexual. And dark.

And now, we sat together in the dark, like always; but this time, the dark was in him.

"Who do you belong to? "
"Pretty Ricky. "
"For how long? "
"For always. "
"Just relax. Close your eyes."

He put a hand gently to my face. My eyelids obeyed the soft downward sweep of the fingers that wanted them closed. He was muttering to himself; or to me; or someone/something that I couldn't see; I couldn't tell. With his fingers he drew an invisible 666 on my forehead. My heart, by now, had to be outside my chest, but I was afraid. I wanted to run shrieking toward the door, but, would he kill me? This was some brand-new stuff; he might just have been crazy enough to sacrifice my body to something. I was already sacrificing it to him. I knew then that he really thought I belonged to him. And I wasn't sure what that meant, but it couldn't have been good. I offered up mental prayers.

"If I get out of here, God, I won't be back."

I'M NOT SURE how long I sat there; how long he tried to put me under his spell. All I knew was that I was wide awake. *Wide awake.* At some point, he stopped chanting or whatever he was doing. We probably had sex; I probably ended up buried somewhere deep in his horrible places; unable to breathe; trying not to hurl; I don't remember. In the mirror that next morning—back at home where nobody ever asked me where I went in the middle of the night and disappeared to for days at a time—I checked my face. I expected to see permanent charcoal-like black sixes staring back at me in reverse. Really. This dummy thought he was the devil's son. And I, the dummy that I was, halfway believed him.

(Pretty Ricky was so . . . pretty . . . really pretty . . . he was tall with curly black shoulder-length hair that he kept corn-rowed back, small slanted, piercing eyes, fair flawless skin and soft thin lips [I think he was half-Caucasian] and ample manhood; even his unibrow was attractive; he was intelligent and semi-talented and kinda nice if you didn't piss him off—aside from his metrosexual-spacey style of dress [which I actually thought was cool, or maybe I just told myself that because I wanted the person in the clothes] and the infrequent bathing, he was fine. The finest thing I would ever have that close to me. I was living a miracle.

And fineness was all that ever mattered, right? We would put up with anything to keep a fine man. I know I would have. I did. Was I insane because I was willing to give up the fineness? Guys just didn't talk to me. When was I ever gonna meet someone fine again? Someone fine that wanted me? Shallowness threatened to succumb my very existence; the very shallowness that I had endured at the hands of others always—that had kept me lonely for so many years—was now in me?)

ON THIS NIGHT, it all died; whatever it was—my Pretty-Ricky-Madness—was gone. Bubbles kept popping all around me everywhere; there was never anything to hold onto. Pretty Ricky wasn't solid; from the beginning I knew this; but I buried it. I told myself I had been brainwashed. When you're used to being the ugly friend; the one who gets picked last or not at all; when someone pretty wants you it's like the sky opening up and raining endless money all over you in a season of dryness. Pretty Ricky was my endless money. And that night, in less than three minutes . . . he just wasn't endless money anymore.

(Bear with me, please—forgive my inconsistency—my memories are a deluge right now . . .

Pretty kept his nails square and razor sharp, just long enough to dig into skin and leave marks while he imprinted his invisible marks on the wombs of those who belonged to him. I had those signature lines everywhere. I had grown used to pain, pretending that discomfort was pleasure, dishonest enough to keep such company, always hoping that it would change—that, sometimes, it would be about me.

But then there was the time when Pretty saved me from contracting chlamydia. He had offered me to his friend, Giovanni [the girl that Giovanni had just met and brought up from the block would not submit to his advances. She left just as quickly as she had come and he remained behind, aroused and ticked off. Pretty felt sorry for him]. Pretty made him wear a condom.

Weeks later, we discovered that the same guy had infected my girlfriend Zaina. She lived with my family and me.; I had introduced her to Pretty. We all hung out on my first night with him—separate actions, same bed. Lucky me, to end up with the uninfected partner. Unlucky Zaina, having me as a friend. I found out several months later that Zaina's contagion did not stop Pretty Ricky from partaking of her body. Never mind her discomfort. He had no condom, so he fashioned himself a garbage bag toga and treated her to a Pretty Ricky selfish special. I'm not kidding. This, the morning after he had introduced her to other things that she should not know, with me right there, participating and not protecting her, listening to her cry and lying quietly while he stroked her hair and pretended that he was not the same as the men who had molested her/me. I was sixteen and she was fourteen.)

My three-month Pretty-high became the puff of smoke it should have been in the first place. On that first afternoon back on The Concourse when he gently removed my glasses from my face—when the whole world came into focus and he gave me temporary sight and took away every negative word anyone had ever burned into me—it was all just another lie in a different way to pin me down on another level. He wanted me in chains. Tonight, when he yelled at me, despite the miasma that had held me all those months, the chains loosened up. When he went there with the sixes, the chains broke.

I went to see him a few more times, at his beckoning. There were always a few more times for me, anyway, to see if I could hold on, if I could stay even though it was scary and it hurt. A few more times usually let me know. I was supposed to come back to braid his hair in a couple of days. I used to love putting my hands in that long, curly, dirty hair. I went to the library with my best friend and her boyfriend instead. I never thought I would miss being the third wheel. It was the lesser of two evils.

Pretty called me and blasted me.

"Now you're not going to see me until I think you deserve to!"

If he could have seen my face, he would probably have slapped me. I was already done. There was no way—I don't care how pretty—I ever wanted to be near him. I danced with a lot of dangerous things. Before that night, I imagined a life ever after with this long-haired, thigh-high-boot-wearin', unibrowed, unkempt whatever-he-was. But the devil had shown me his face. I was not dancin' with him, not anymore and not on purpose.

But he wouldn't go quietly. He would be M.I.A. for weeks and then he would pop up. Just checkin' to see if I was keepin' it tight. It had been nearly two months. I was dating Greg again; he was my first, technically. Finally, the relationship was working, and I didn't want anyone else. Pretty was angry. He came to my house in the middle of the night and Edith let him in. He choked me a little, made me do some stupid, nasty stuff, and then used his manhood to show me who I belonged to. He talked about himself for an eternity and left, stopping short at the door.

"If you ever see Greg again, I'll kill him. And you."

I called Greg that following afternoon and told him about the encounter. He asked me if I had had sex with Pretty. I didn't answer. I wasn't sure if he meant that night, or ever. He hung up on me.

That night, I swallowed every pill of every bottle of medication that my mother had on her dresser. I left a really long letter. That was Christmas Eve and I spent Jesus's birthday weekend in Bronx Lebanon Hospital hallucinating mice and water bugs, having my stomach pumped (they made me swallow liquid charcoal and some thick, yellowish clear stuff that tasted like bile. I had had beef lo mein earlier that night; apparently, I had swallowed it whole; the contents of my stomach revealed noodles and beef strips that had not been chewed; it would be twenty-two years before I ever ate lo mein again), strapped to a wheelchair (they didn't believe me about the mice and the water bugs, but my mind said they were there; they were everywhere). I didn't die and Greg left me because he thought I was crazy.

In May of 1987, Pretty found me again. I told my friends to go home without me and I stood with him on the corner of The Concourse and East Tremont. We walked to the park, I listened to him sing (ilk!) and talk about himself. I gave him what he asked for, right there in the park. I didn't even want him. I was just scared to say no.

Then came November 1987. I was dating a guy named Derrick. We had just left his apartment, I kissed him good-bye, and was about to climb into a taxi. Pretty Ricky pulled up beside us in a white Lincoln, called me his famous *Priscilla*, I said "Hi," and ducked into my cab. For Pretty Ricky, that was just as good as being completely ignored.

He waited until we drove down the block and intercepted my ride. No crashing, just threats, enough to make me get out and go with him. He drove me around.

"I miss you so much."

A few questions for me, and then it was all about him.

"I miss the way you would kiss me all over . . . please . . ."
(Oh damn.)
"Just this one time . . . "
"I can't. "
"Please? I miss you so much. "
"I can't. I need to go home. I have a boyfriend . . . "
"You belong to me. "
"I have to go. "
"Not until you . . ."

His voice was soft, but there was a knowing in his pretty eyes that warned that it might not stay that way for long. He parked somewhere in Soundview near the field that nobody would walk through because it was supposedly infested with crazy disease-carrying mosquitoes. He got it; he always did. The whole time, in the car—while I leaned forward over the reclined passenger seat and his tall eager body spooned my short reluctant form, as he grunted and whispered mendacious words that stole my peace, as I tried to figure out why he wanted it when it didn't want him and why he couldn't tell that I was faking, all the while a dirge playing in my soul—of all the thoughts that ran through my mind, what stood out the most was how disgusting I was. Why didn't I fight? Why didn't I just take the chance that he might not hold to his threats? How did he manage to do this every time?

He drove me home; still talking about himself; still telling me he loved me like nothing ever happened. I had to go upstairs, sit in the faces of the people I lived with and tell them that I allowed myself to be taken advantage of.[16] Again. I couldn't cry; there were no tears left. I tried to force them out, but all I could do was laugh. How easy it was for me to accept this. How ashamed I was that these kinds of things kept happening to me. Surely I was a magnet. It had to be me, because there was always someone new. Once it's on you it's hard to get it off; they can see you comin'. I was a punk; I should have been fighting for mine. DeVonni and Keisha looked at me like they didn't know what to think. I could almost hear their thoughts:

Did he really make her do this, or did she want it?

I don't blame them. I took the next day off from work. I wanted to take a day off from everybody, especially my boyfriend Derrick. I didn't even want him to touch me anymore. I felt like I had betrayed him.

That was late winter. Spring came and went and then there was summer and Pretty was visible in the old neighborhood all the time—much more than when I kept regular company with him. But I only saw him, it seemed, when I was with Derrick. He always thought he could dis the next man and get away with it. He thought I would walk away from Derrick and come to him. I didn't. He would say things to me while we walked by, but he wouldn't come near me.

"Bitch, you think you can play me? I will kill your whole family!"

I looked back, I snickered and Derrick and I kept walking. I got some threatening phone calls after that, but I never yielded. I had finally broken free.

So again, at age twenty-two, six years after I had met and defiled myself with him, I sensed Pretty Ricky's essence. I was on the corner of Burnside and Jerome Avenues, waiting for a ride, and was on a pay phone talking to DeVonni. Red movement in my peripheral drew my attention to the

---

[16] I was still living with Aunt Delores an' them

left. There was a man on a red motorcycle. He removed his helmet of the same color. He was staring. His smirk was familiar. Nothing clicked until he spoke . . .

"Don't I know you? "
"No. "
"Yes, I do. "
"No, you don't. "
"Yes, I do, Priscilla. "
"DeVonni, it's Pretty Ricky. "
"Nisey, leave now . . ." (She was scared for me. She didn't have to be.)
"Do you want me to call the police? "
"No, I got this. I'll call you back."

He stepped off the bike. Smirk intact, he gaited to me slowly, towering in a black skin-tight T-shirt, black straight-legged jeans, and black Timberlands. He was thicker, muscular. His chest was . . . amazing. He had a Caesar haircut. *So fine*. I mean ridiculous. Finer than I'd ever seen him. *Prettier*. I wanted to lick him. And I wanted to reach up six foot-three or five, or how ever tall he was, and punch him in the face, too. Oddly, I wasn't afraid. He spoke again.

"Your skin looks beautiful, thanks to me."

He reached out to touch my face. I pulled away. He believed that all the semen he had me ingest all those years ago was a treatment for blackheads. He made sure I never wasted any.

I stared him down. I had to look up to him to do it, but I was strangely confident. I wanted to rock his world, teach him a lesson, make him fall in love with me, and leave him dangling. But I knew better . . . I was still a hot mess and a novice at a game he had seemingly mastered. Another romp with Pretty would have taken me out.

"Why did you tell people that the reason you tried to kill yourself was because of me? "
"It was because of you. You hurt me. You made me feel trapped. I would never have had a life because of you. "

"But I loved you. I know I did a lot of things that were wrong, and I'm sorry. But God has truly changed me . . ."

I listened to his unconvincing spiel. My ride pulled up in his pretty white Lincoln. This was Stacey—a six foot three chocolaty *oh-my-goodness*. He was an alcoholic and his pores gave him up to that truth. Bumping uglies with him was like swimming in a barrel of Jack Daniels. He would soon spread the news of our episodes all over Gunhill Road (where he lived) and Riker's Island[17] (where he worked)—symptoms, usually, of a lack of instrument or skill. Stacey suffered of both. He was no better for me than Pretty, but at least he'd never own me.

Stacey's boys were in the back of his car. They climbed out, wild-eyed, no doubt high on something, looking like they wanted to hurt somebody. Like a pretty boy.

"You aah'ite? He botherin' you? "
"Nah, I'm okay. "
"You sure? "
"Yeah."

I walked away with Stacey and his crew. Pretty shouted out his pager number.

"Yo' Priscilla-call me!"

So fine . . . don't get distracted, Girl.

I am good with numbers, names, dates; I can recall conversations and events verbatim. I thought I had memorized that number; I don't know why I wanted to. And I did try to call him.

Something scrambled whatever part of my brain was in charge of number memory. Because I didn't get it right.

---

[17] Stacey was a Corrections Officer @ Riker's Island.

Suicide Attempt

Journal, December 12, 2009; Regarding December 24-26, 1986

I CRAWLED INTO THE ROOM where Edith was sleeping. I wasn't distraught; I just didn't really want to be found dead. She sounded annoyed when I told her I had taken all of her pills.

"What'choo do dat for? "
"I don't know." I was crying, but not really, and a little dizzy.
"Y'all kids git on my damn nerves!" Edith sucked her teeth and got up off the cot she was sleeping on.

I was pretty messed up when Denise, my friend Latisha's aunt, and Edith walked me down the block to Bronx Lebanon Hospital. I was talkin' all kinds of crazy and laughing to myself. Denise kept talkin' to me, tryin' to keep me from passin' out. I wasn't wearing my glasses and my head was in a crazy fog world. It felt really good, but my body was boneless, it seemed; my legs wanted to ribbon under me like honey drizzling on a ham. It was Christmas Day, about one o'clock in the morning.

AFTER THE EMERGENCY ROOM (where my stomach was pumped[18]), I was transferred to the Fulton Avenue division of Bronx Lebanon Hospital. I stayed up all night, my mind restored except for the nagging hallucination of one

---
[18] pp. 63

mouse. Earlier, I had seen dozens of them and a gang of water bugs. The doctors and nurses insisted there were none, but you couldn't convince me otherwise.
BEFORE THE NURSES LEFT MY ROOM that night (after they hit me with a barrage of health questions and queries as to why I had attempted suicide; after I vehemently insisted that I had not been hallucinating, that I had actually seen what I thought I saw), I overheard them discussing all the medications I had taken. They said that one in particular was a water pill called Inderal. I played with that name in my mind over the years: *end-her-all . . . I almost ended it all with Inderal . . . how funny that was . . .*

The nurses said that the amount of Inderal I had consumed should have paralyzed me for life. I wonder what the angel guarding my silly behind was thinking that night . . . *Lord, you keep sending me to block for this nut; seriously, what do you see in her?*

I was in the same hospital room *and* bed that I had stayed in for eighteen days with Corwin's gift of PID; and I was finally aware that the bugs and mice that I had seen earlier had not really been there, and I didn't want to freak out the girl in the bed next to me; the mouse I thought I saw was crawling above her headboard. I just stared at it—nervous and itching to cry out "Look at that mouse!" remembering that it wasn't real, feeling helpless (who wants to lose their mind, even if only for a few hours, and know that it's been lost *while* it's still kinda lost?)—until I eventually fell asleep.

THE NEXT DAY I MET with the hospital's child psychologist on call. He was a Caucasian man, he sat in a tiny room about two doors down from my room. He was surrounded by stacks of paper, his head down, eyes glued to what I guessed was my file. He didn't look up from the papers as he told me to sit down. My therapy session began. I stared at the top of his head where hair-gelled strands, borrowed from what was left on the sides, draped reluctantly.

"Why'd you try to kill yourself? "
"There's this guy named Pretty Ricky. He threatened me and— "
"So why didn't you just tell someone? "
"I didn't know anyone would list— "
"What do you mean you didn't know anyone would listen? "
"I meant exactly what I said. "
"Why didn't you tell your mother?"

He was still looking at his paperwork, his tone cold and unsympathetic, not waiting for or content with my answers. Was he even writing this stuff down? He was shooting off questions like players at basketball drills, like cops trying to trick an innocent brown-boy-at-the-wrong-place-at-wrong-time into confession. Was this therapy or central booking?

"Cuz she doesn't care about me. She— "
"That doesn't make any sense. "
"Yeah, well, that's what it is."

I was a little annoyed by then. Okay, I was ticked off, but I was holdin' it down. I wanted to slap him upside his comb-over and tell him to come live my nightmare for five minutes and see what kinda crap he'd end up OD-ing on. But I didn't. I let him rag me like I let everybody rag me every day up until that moment, three days after my seventeenth birthday.

"Well, next time tell somebody. "
"Yeah, okay."
"I'm giving you a referral to see a psychologist. If you don't go every week for the next several weeks, we're gonna have you committed. Do you understand? "
"Uh-huh. "
"Sign this."

I was a minor, but I was signing stuff without Edith present. Stuff was mad-laid-back, no protocol, no rules, it seemed. But I had not yet learned to speak up for myself.

I took the slip of paper and went back to my room. Expletives invaded my membrane. Comb-over boy didn't even want the answers to the questions he asked. He was probably just annoyed that he had to spend Christmas Day in a reject ghetto hospital talking to a ghetto reject.

MY BEST FRIEND JEANNE stopped by to see me for a few minutes. We hadn't seen each other in a while and that was my fault; I had started hangin' with other people and didn't make time for her. It was Christmas, so I didn't expect to see her at all, let alone have her sit with me all day holding my hand. I was really glad to see her, but didn't show it much because she had people with her. She was about to go on a double date with her cousin Helen and their new beaus.

Jeanne and Helen were pretty girls; they always had dates. I was usually a third wheel, a fifth wheel, or a sympathy sidecar, so sitting there in that hospital bed looking at those beautiful girls with their new Christmas clothes made even more evident the waste of time my having swallowed those pills had been. Nothing had changed and, had I died, life would have gone on without me.

"Now, next time," (second time I had heard that in twenty-four hours) Jeanne said, "don't do something like this. Come and talk to me. You know I'm here for you. "

"Okay." (Second time I had said that in twenty-four hours.)

I WENT TO THE PSYCHOLOGIST APPOINTMENTS, but only because they gave me free subway tokens that I cashed in to buy snacks. I had my school subway pass, so I didn't need the tokens.

There were usually three psyches in the room—all young, Caucasian interns wearing white coats. They would smile at first, and then maintain a strange look throughout our sessions—I guess it was the "therapist-look"—like, I knew they were listening, but I didn't get the sense that they really cared and I knew they couldn't relate. But at least, unlike comb-over boy, they looked at me. In fact, I wished they would stop.

After a few weeks of digging me out with questions that didn't really help me find any answers to why my life was so messed up, they asked me if I wanted to participate in a study at New York Presbyterian Hospital. It paid thirty bucks and gave me access to more free subway tokens.

I gave all the details of my adventurous little life to the college student (also Caucasian) who interviewed me every week for the next month. I didn't give two craps what kind of statistics I was being shuffled into. I just wanted my thirty bucks, unmindful that these sessions were not much different than the sexual probings I had once been victim of and later constantly availed myself to.

What no one knew—what I would not reveal until much later in life—was that, when I swallowed all those pills, I did not *really* want to kill myself. I just wanted Pretty Ricky to go away, for Greg to see that I really loved him and, even though I thought I hated her and usually didn't care what she thought of me, I wanted Edith to give a damn.

Edith

Journal Entry, November 2008; Regarding Everything

HER DRESSER AND MEDICINE CABINET were laced with pill bottles. Her teeth were removed when she was thirty-seven; her breasts a year later (in a botched breast reduction, her ampleness was cut down [literally, it seems, considering the way she was put back together with vitiligo-like scarring all around her areola] from an G-cup to a B), her uterus was gone in another six. She practically disappeared. She never asked any questions. She just let them tell her what she needed—for herself, and for us.

I know this from the glasses I got at age five that she never let me take off my face (although they were only for reading), the series of allergy shots I got at age six (I wasn't allergic to anything), and the pills she let the doctor prescribe me at age fourteen to treat bacne (back acne that could have been resolved if I had simply given up soda). The pills made me high, but they did not cure the bacne. But this was Edith's cure for heartache.

The attention she got from her peers, when she got attention, was self-diminishing. After the mailman left and the social security checks were spent, so was their time with her. She was everybody's errand runner and babysitter, her compensation being a few bucks and the opportunity to be used often. So letting doctors take her apart and use her children as guinea pigs made her feel important, I guess.

SHE HAD A VOICE THAT NOBODY WANTED TO HEAR. How could she love her children? She barely had herself. After the adults finished with her, all that was left was strength to pick up the pieces. Maybe.

There was no time in between to find herself. And the babies kept coming. And she depended on everyone except them to make her feel needed.

I learned early how to use the children—the babies—to make me feel needed. To substitute laundry, cooking, and cleaning for takeout, Toys'R'Us and VHS marathons; to spend valuable homework-help time masquerading my pain in laughter-drag at G-rated movies; to snuggle up in between them and breathe in their innocence; their heads nestled against my chest, fingers entwined with mine, feeding me life; every moment cherished and temporary; my spirit craving them deeply during work hours; rushing home and doing it over and over again amidst the criticism of the old mothers and the ones who thought they knew what it was like to be me . . .

Edith never learned that. They never taught her anything, they just pushed her out there. The world taught her. They saw her coming and they leeched. She had nothing. And they even took that.

NOBODY SAW WHO SHE REALLY WAS. Not even I. Although mostly ignored, I became what was needed to unleash what she could not show them. She wanted to tell them that they hurt her, but she learned somewhere that they wouldn't listen. So she would tell me. She did not talk with words. Mostly it was silence. Neglect. Punches. She needed someplace to put those things.

Why me, when there were four of us? I didn't know it then. I took her for a ho' with no respect for my daddy's love. But it was the one who misappropriated her body who did not defer. He did what the others—the ones that knew her—he did what they did only he left something tangible for her to hate. Had I known what I was, maybe I would have been like the children of drug addicts.

Maybe, once, I was. They're the ones who extend endless worship to parents who would sell them for a rock. My mother was no drug addict.

Mishandled, she was. But I found it hard to love her. All I could see was the empty refrigerator and the molesters and the manipulating friends and crackhead bedmates; the times when she would stuff her face with Honey Buns and Twinkies and tell us she had no money to buy us dinner. I didn't notice the fragile and broken girl/woman whose only hope was in a Twinkie because her destiny was defined in her youth by unsupervised misfits who carelessly passed her around until she was confused. Lost. No way back for her.

No one would blame me for thinking ill of her. Much of my adult life mimicked hers. Resentment magnified when I saw *her* in *me*. I chased brick walls. I always saw her face as I was running, and I would curse her name as I bashed my face against the mortar. Sometimes I'd pause and a moment of my time would ache in her place. And then I would be back to chasing brick walls. Always blaming her. Knowing that somewhere along the line I was the one who did not choose the way out.

SHE HAD TO HAVE BEEN BORN WITH REAL LOVE. Because she was naïve, trusting, and pure, she couldn't possibly hate. But it must have run dry. How could she continue to love when never given a chance?

"She ain't that stupid, she' know what she' doin'!"

If I could erase every thought I had of her then. All the back talk and the judgment. I remember making her cry. I'm sure it wasn't about me; I'm sure I was the feather atop a very large pile. But she cried and I told myself I didn't care. But as I watched her dry her tears, my pride-muffled heart whispered deafeningly, but I couldn't say sorry because I only wanted to think about what she had done to me to please the others; what she hadn't done for me to please the others; what she had ignored to please the others; all the pain she fed me every day.

That voice that nobody wanted to hear was in those tears, trying to show how helpless she was. I was eleven years old. I didn't want to hear. I had stopped hoping for a mother who would mother me. I didn't know how to hear the tears. I had cried so many on my own; ones that she never saw; never heard; voiceless; just like hers.

Maybe she could hear but her power was gone. Oh, to get that day back and wrap my weak arms around her neck and say it till it all rewinds: *I know what they do; they do it to me, too; together we can take it back; together we can close the doors; together we can do it all over again; together let's run where we don't know; together it will be better than this* . . .

The Way He Loved Me (7 Abortions Part I)

Journal, March 2009, Regarding April 1990

> *Meander-n. A loop in a river or stream or a series of such loops; a winding, convolute course or path.*

NO MATTER WHAT HE SAID, I had a counterargument. I'm sure that he could see that I was scared and confused, but I was ticking him off. He was only trying to find a solution. I just never imagined the solution to be abortion.

He had had enough. The first slap came without warning although, by now, I should have recognized the shift in the atmosphere. He was yelling. His hulking form leaning over me, my body sitting on the sofa, face looking up at him with pleading eyes, his eyes glazed over with pain and exasperation, mouth shouting mists of angry saliva showering my face, no regard for my pitiful countenance. I drew my knees to my chest and buried my face there. My hands went up to cover my head as the rain came. My crying wasn't so much from the pain of his strong open hands crashing against my thighs—my arms, my head—as it was for the confusion that crashed against my brain. How could I be pregnant *again*? The cycle was fresh, but it was en force. I was a full-blown statistic.

I DIDN'T HAVE PLANS. I was Q's mommy and I was going to be a famous singer. One great blessing, one great idea, but no plans. So life navigated me. Every element therein dictated who I would become. In this encounter with Baby's Daddy #1, I was about to be given new instructions that I would follow to the letter, no questions asked. I was going to mutilate my unborn. Baby's Daddy #1 had his own problems. I nursed this idea. I took his physical way of loving me as punishment for surreptitious unfaithfulness; my lies about how I occupied my after-work time; the time when he thought I was at the gym battling baby fat.

I was a conditional lover and I knew that I was always going to cheat on him. I gave most of myself to him for as long as it took to convince him to love me my way. I'm not really sure what that was, I didn't really know what I was looking for, I just knew I needed someone. This was the beginning of my manufacture of love—my attempt at creating a whole man from pieces. This kind of living hurts so many people . . . even those who aren't here yet.

Baby's Daddy #1 was so beautiful. Not just his ebonite—his firm physical blackness—but his heart. He was not necessarily a conditional lover, like me. What I saw was a lover who learned by watching. His stories are not mine to share, but I can say that he watched pain; he watched suffering; he watched infidelity; he watched violence; he watched death. He seemed to get by on what he had. If sex was the way, he did it. If money was the way, he gave it.

When we first hooked up, I was fresh out of my relationship with Derrick, looking for some arms to wrap myself in, a chest to lay my head against. I don't think he was looking for anything. I told him I didn't need exclusivity, and he was cool with that. He let me take the lead and when he made no moves to explore my secret places, I counted it a threat to my femininity and proceeded to make it sexual.

THREE WEEKS AFTER OUR FIRST DATE (which was really my body pressed up against his in the dark on a bench on the grounds of Patterson Projects in The Bronx), we conceived in the darkness of a bedroom right next to the one in which he was conceived and born in his parents' first-floor Mitchell Projects apartment. I knew nothing of his plans for life or future, but I'm sure it didn't include having a baby at the age of twenty-one.

But whatever they were, he laid down his pursuits to walk with me through our first pregnancy. I remember meeting him in the waiting room after my clinic visit to confirm what my missing period had already established. I knelt before him and assured him that I didn't need his help; I did not expect his love and I would not hold him to father a child he did not ask for. I would do it alone. The eyes in his lowered head remained glued to his folded hands; an incomprehensible smile rested upon his face.

He was a gentleman. Clearly in pain from his own life's journey and not afraid to share his tears, he silently committed to be someone to me; whomever he could be. He had lost his job and all he had was someone to care for. We were fine as long as I didn't ask to be married. He didn't want to get married. But he came to the table with what he had and he was good to me.

And then I hit a nerve that sent him back to what he had learned. He had trusted me not only with his body and a covenant of two with an unspoken promise to keep it between us, but he had trusted me with his sorrow. It was too much for me. I didn't want his sorrow without a wedding ring. I had sorrow of my own.

So I betrayed him. I gave myself to another and, even though he had no proof, I know his spirit knew. One time in particular, I hadn't even cheated. I had merely made contact with a prospect and left evidence. An accidentally tape-recorded conversation, my susurrous voice playing phone games with a used-to-be-lover. I came home to a raging black ball of fire.

He dragged me to the bedroom by my hair, made me listen to the tape, and slapped me every time I tried to speak; he would ask me a question, pause for my answer, and then hit me with a brain-rattling open hand before I could get the words out. He was used to women fawning over him, not cheating on him.

THIS WAS THE FIRST TIME HE HAD EVER HURT ME. I went to the bathroom and combed through what was left of my hair. It grew back and we survived my first spanking; but he found it real easy to hit me after that.

A couple of weeks later, it was a slap to the left ear that left me partially deaf for about three days. Another night he pushed me down the hallway. My feet left the ground and my head hit the floor. I blacked out and awakened to him holding and rocking me back and forth, massaging the back of my head. He said sorry. There were also a couple of black eyes—one complete with a broken blood vessel in the white of my a right eye and ring scratch to the temple—that I covered up with my bangs and told people came from a baseball that Baby Q threw and accidentally hit me in the eye.

I HAD THE ABORTION; it was my first. And each time we found my womb full with another accident (condoms just weren't his thing [I got cursed out for insisting that he use them; it was, after all, my job to ensure that I didn't get pregnant], pulling out stole from the experience, and I just couldn't remember to take a pill), I didn't even bother to present a scenario. I just pulled out my low-cost health insurance card and made an appointment at my favorite House of TOP.[19]

Together, we decided to abort five babies; at least one of whom I'm certain wasn't even his. And, in between, life went on as usual. I got most of my beatings on Sundays. The subconscious turning over in his mind of my having a job to go to every day and his having to spend fifty hours a week at home with our son lit arguments from the most simple of matches: I spent too much time in the mirror, I stared too long at an attractive actor on television, my dress was too short, too tight, too low cut, or all three. I didn't know when to shut up, though. My mouth would still be running right into the unleashing of blows.

I remember Q, even at the age of two, trying to console me. He saw too much and, even though I loved him achingly, the fear of being alone didn't allow me to love him enough to leave our comfortable little situation. I didn't find out until he was almost nine years old (five years out of my relationship with his dad; two years into a mental nightmare with Baby's Daddy #2) that my baby boy was scared for me; protecting me in his little heart; carrying a burden much too heavy for a child.

Nearly twenty years later, I have a few physical reminders of the poor choices I made. I am not angry or holding myself prisoner, though; just glad to be alive; glad that Baby's Daddy #1 and I got away from each other and escaped what could have been: the meander—the loops that always seemed to dump us into the same place: nowhere.

---

[19] T.O.P. (Termination of Pregnancy) is another medical term for abortion

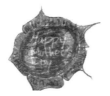

A Rational Conversation about Child Support

Date: Thu, 1 Feb 2007 07:42:47-0800
From: <ql@are_you_kidding_me.com>
Subject: Hi . . .
To: <km@nope_i'm_dead_serious.net>

I wanted to speak with you, again, about getting regular financial help with K . . .

I am doing my best to care for our daughter with the resources I have; but it's just not enough.

I bear the bulk of the care for K on so many levels—emotionally, spiritually, physically, and financially . . . I'm not sure why you don't want to give me money on a regular basis . . . I have never given you reason to think that I wouldn't use it to care for K.

It's just not expedient for me to have to come to you and ask every time I need something for K. Sometimes you don't come through right away and I'm forced to keep asking you and wait until you decide you want to do it. It's more than just an inconvenience; it's demeaning. You probably don't care about my feelings at all and I don't fault you for that, but getting help from you for our daughter shouldn't be an emotional ordeal.

All I'm asking for is $250 per month—$62.50 per week—on the 15 of every month. Even that is not much; but it will help. Please consider it prayerfully and get back to me . . . I just need more help from you with our daughter. I pray you'll reconsider your decision. Thanks for hearing me out . . . I'm not trying to start a fight.

QuYahni

<km@nope_i'm_dead_serious.net> wrote:

Hey. Got your message . . .

I can understand your position. But with all due respect, you know your life is your own and you made your choices.

Come on now, with all due respect, this is your bed. You're just feeling the pains financially. The thing is, come on now, let's be real and honest, less kids, less money. You have x amount of kids, so of course, you're going to have to spend more money than the person with only one child, it's basic math.

I only have one child. With, or without her, my rent, my food bill, would be the same. If the rolls were reversed, and you only had one child the scenario would be the same as mine is now. One kid, less expenses.

Come on D, we've had this talk before. It's not right, nor fair. However, the good part is, without fail, whenever you've asked for whatever, I never hesitated, nor made you feel unwelcomed. It's all good. Our daughter needs—she has a mother and a father, so we make do in what we have.

Job, you have a nine to five. I, on the other, had still hustle. No steady gig. I have to go out and get it! I've been blessed, and I'm tryin' to stay that way. So in light of all that's been said, let's keep the peace. You know me, don't start nothin' . . . well, you know the rest.

You have a big family babe, you want—you got it.

I mean no harm or disrespect. This is just the paths we're on, and still it can be pleasant.

Thank you.

One kid Big K.

———

Date: Fri, 2 Feb 2007 07:04:35-0800
From: <ql@are_you_kidding_me.com>
Subject: Please Listen . . .
To: <km@nope_i'm_dead_serious.net>

What you're saying about my family and my choices have absolutely nothing to do with this. I'm not asking you to take care of them, and I'm not even asking you to provide an equal share of K's living expenses; just a small portion.

———

<km@nope_i'm_dead_serious.net> wrote:

With all due respect, once again you're not seeing the truth, just your point.

Tell you what, take away your kids, with the exception of K, and see the savings. Let me have more kids, and watch the spending; if I have it.

You're asking monies to help you, not K. Come on now. Take K out of the equation, your rent is still the same, your food bill the same.

Or, if I'm overlooking the fact, if you wish for her to stay with me, let's work something out . . .

That might be something we should look into.

Any—who, what can I say? You feel how you feel, but setting that aside, I wish you could see the facts and logic.

Well, just keeping the line of communication open . . .

———

Date: Mon, 5 Feb 2007 12:48:36-0800
From: <ql@are_you_kidding_me.com>
Subject: RE: Please Listen . . .
To: <km@nope_i'm_dead_serious.net>

Okay, again, it's not about me; it's about K—just K; but I already know that, no matter what I say, you're only going to see it your way . . .

What you're saying is, rather than give me $62.50 per week, you would rather uproot her again and have her come live with you. How logical is that? Anyway, I'm not going back and forth with this . . .

—

<km@nope_i'm_dead_serious.net> wrote:

Wow, what can I say? You know . . . What? I guess you'll never bow down to the truth and logic. Your essence or anger is all in your letter; however, I will not let the indignation I feel get the better.

Denise, you are wrong and way outta line. Come on . . .

You just don't, or won't see.

K needs for nothing. She has two places to live, food to eat! Hey, if you wanna see receipts, I guarantee you, yours do not match mine. And being that I don't shop at those cheap cookies stores, I'm paying a lot more.

You buy what you buy. I don't question you, or your taste; which is questionable; sorry, had to throw that in there; and that, was joking, I think.

Any—who, all can be well, if you keep your cool and faith. My goal is always for peace in the universe.

1 L U V.

From: <ql@are_you_kidding_me.com>
To: <km@nope_i'm_dead_serious.net>
Sent: Tue, February 6, 2007 3:52:08 p.m.
Subject: Cool . . .

I'm not angry, nor is my faith in The One Who made me shaken, at all. Thank you for hearing me out . . .

QuYahni

Every Rose Has Thorns

Journal Entry, March 2009; Regarding February 1996-December 1999

THIS IS ONE STORY that Denise had a very hard time telling. She could tell you real easy about being physically violated. But talking about being beat down by someone in the spirit is another struggle entirely.

With him, she could not win with words. It was just like being raped each and every time. Years after she had left him and moved on to what was really meant for her, he was still able to beat and molest her with unjust taunting and piercing lies that he created deep within his psyche; lies that had become truth to him. They had a child together; she was always going to be available to him. No matter how she fought, he still had her pinned down, broken and exposed, bleeding and waiting for death. She had to decide a million times over that she wasn't going to subject herself to it anymore. She thought she was done making that decision, just as she had thought the first time she left him so many years before . . .

(When you get out, stay out. Don't ever go back. Don't even look back.)

SHE HAD LET HIM BACK IN and their lovemaking had changed. She tried so hard to enjoy what was taking place. He was no different than before. He was always gentle, there appeared to be amazing love inside of him when this happened between them, it was the only time that he seemed real, open, vulnerable. But *Denise* was different. She saw faces that weren't his. Her body felt like she was under the weight of many probing, self-seeking, nasty men. In reality (in spirit), she truly was. And his transgression was by far the worst (some had physically abused her, some had taken advantage and left, but he tormented her soul); just bad enough to make him pay for the offenses of them all.

SHE KNEW HE NEEDED HER desperately to need him. From what she was told, there was a woman of significance who had cut off his penis, tossed it somewhere, and left him to find it and sew it back on himself. Metaphorically speaking, of course. It was said that she had done this often.

And he only seemed "normal" when Denise was doing the same. So she did. She wanted so badly to treat him like a man—like a valuable man—but she couldn't. Before her, he had spent too much time alone, creating a character who would appear strong and complete yet, having no approving impression of himself, built a plinth to maintain his weak self-image; a plinth comprised of the degradation and debasing of weaker people . . . of women, mostly . . . of Denise who, briefly, but long enough to sear her psyche, became his live-in punching bag.

PEOPLE WANTED TO KNOW WHY. *Why him?* They looked on his outward appearance—a hefty frame, careless dress—and dismissed him as unworthy. Denise never looked; she didn't think. She fell in love with *la sonrisa de su juventud*; she emptied her life into his ears; he listened; he smiled, sometimes kissed her, offering occasional flattery and superficial interjections; there was no real substance to his conversation; even so, she felt safe.

She didn't know that he was storing her secrets for later use. He was going to kill her with them.

He didn't know how to love her when she was truly loving him. Being good to him meant compromising the already diminutive sense of value she was clinging to. By the time he was done twisting her vision of herself (and she was eight months pregnant by then, his seed growing inside of her, experiencing her every pain, hearing Father's words tear into Mother, becoming one with the struggle it would be born into), she wanted to kill herself.

To give her heart to him again meant certain death. So she had to hurt him, instead. And he didn't care; as long as she was volatile and confused, she would be too ashamed to keep company with anyone who would provide the encouragement she needed to break free of him; she would need him only; so he let her believe that she had some power.

SHE REMEMBERED A BREAKING POINT . . . she was on her knees. She was like Hannah[20]—in so much pain, but not an answer came to life. There were no words left. So when she opened her mouth, a language that she had never spoken before—one that made no sense to her—came ripping out. She thought she was losing her mind. She tried to stop herself, but every time she spoke (. . .) her prayers were in her heart, and her lips were moving, but her voice was not heard.[21]

She implored relief—she wanted to be free of this man. She wanted to be free of loving wrong, expecting a man to produce newness from dry-old-deadness, looking to be filled up by someone who was so very empty.

> *"God grabbed me. God's Spirit took me up and set me down in the middle of an open plain strewn with bones. He led me around and among them—a lot of bones! There were bones all over the plain—dry bones, bleached by the sun.*
> *He said to me, "[Daughter] [. . .], can these bones live?"*
> *I said, "Master God, only you know that."*
> *He said to me, "Prophesy over these bones: 'Dry bones, listen to the Message of God!'"*
> *God, the Master, told the dry bones, "Watch this: I'm bringing the breath of life to you and you'll come to life. I'll attach sinews to you, put meat on your bones, cover you with skin, and breathe life into you. You'll come alive and you'll realize that I am God!"*
> *I prophesied just as I'd been commanded. As I prophesied, there was a sound and, oh, rustling! The bones moved and came together, bone to bone. I kept watching. Sinews formed, then muscles on the*

---

[20] 1 Samuel 1
[21] 1 Samuel 1:13

> *bones, then skin stretched over them. But they had no breath in them.*[22]

AND SHE GOT OUT; went not far, but far enough to stay away. But she wasn't free. And her body got lonely. It got lonely enough to make her believe that she could change his brand of love. She was so confused and she didn't care. She pretended, too. She pretended that while she was in his arms and he was all over her, it was all right. It was so temporary, but it was good enough to risk the hateful invectives, the deliberate mental detention. It was so worth it. *Because while she was in his arms and he was all over her*, she turned him into her savior, her protector, her daddy. She made him everything she needed to relive her childhood the way it should have been. Oh, it was so amazing—you had to be there—he said such amorous things to her while she was beneath him . . . he lifted her high and made her deep-poetry sing . . . he made her believe.

And no matter how painful the reality—because she had prescience that flowed when she wrote the things she wished; she wished for love; she knew he would score her to her very essence—when she came down and he showed her the truth (he did not really love her), as much as she fought to let him go, fatuous longings kept her. She stayed for the euphoria of their playtime.

> *He said to me, "Prophesy to the breath. Prophesy [. . .] Tell the breath, 'God, the Master, says, Come from the four winds. Come, breath. Breathe on these slain bodies. Breathe life!'"*
>
> *So I prophesied, just as he commanded me. The breath entered them and they came alive . . .*
>
> *Then God said to me, "{Daughter} of man, these bones are the whole house of Israel. Listen to what they're saying: 'Our bones are dried up, our hope is gone, there's nothing left of us.'*
>
> *Therefore, prophesy. Tell them, 'God, the Master, says: I'll dig up your graves and bring you out alive . . . I'll breathe my life into you and you'll live'"*[23]

---

[22] Ezekiel 37:1-8, The Message Bible
[23] Ezekiel 37:9-14(The Message Bible)

SO HERE THEY WERE, AGAIN. But this time, there was Jesus in her and there were legions of demons all around. The legions ran through his body—with every man from childhood to now that had ever taken her without her permission—to conquer her; but conviction stood strong and made her want nothing less than The One Who had truly saved her.

Not overnight, but over lonely nights and busy days and dips and dives into unknown places, searching still; that reality, that prayer of freedom and peace, becomes flesh more so every day. She's like new again . . . and her memory sometimes creeps to when she gave him things he could not handle . . . sometimes she remembers . . . no matter how beautiful or pleasant the odor, every rose has thorns . . .

Number Six (7 Abortions, Part II)

Journal Entry, Spring 2009; Regarding October 1995

> *"I've seen sonograms with the baby pulling away from the instruments that are introduced into the vagina."*
>
> —*Carol Everett, former abortion clinic owner*[24]

I WOKE UP CRYING AND CLUTCHING MY STOMACH, yelling and tearing at my belly, praying that it was a dream. Days earlier, I had been listening to a Christian radio station. I was looking for some comfort, something to ease my mind while I let my decision sink in. The announcer was talking about abortions.

> . . . *a handheld syringe is used to abort a child from six weeks to twelve weeks of age . . . works by creating its own vacuum/suction . . . used and reused millions of times a year around the world . . . it has a very weak vacuum . . . the child is ripped apart slowly . . . brain and tissue and sinew . . .*[25]

The description boomed and echoed off the walls of my friend's apartment. I was alone except for the radio and the life in my belly. I went out onto the terrace, the announcer's voice following me, beating against

---

[24] http://www.youtube.com/watch?v=uo6uYo6Yooo
[25] http://abortioninstruments.com/index_instruments2.html

the back of my head. No more effective than the graphic illustrations I had seen in the women's medical books I used to read as a teen. This was number six and, while I was sick of the cycle, I had no intentions of handling things any differently.

But I was not prepared to hurt or care. I have had laminaria insertion, a procedure that is used to abort fetuses that are more than three and a half months gestation; I sat for an entire day in a separate waiting area, watching soap operas and chatting with other unwitting and numbing accomplices while my cervix dilated and I waited for the surgeons to crush and extract life from my womb. The proceeding excruciating cramps were a small price to pay for the renewed liberation to offer myself to someone else who would possibly deposit yet another someone that I had no desire to nurture. It was okay as long as I waited four weeks, of course, so as to avoid infection of another kind . . .

Why was this any different? The nurses threatened to strap me to the gurney. They had asked me several times to calm down; I was upsetting the other patients. But I couldn't stop my mouth from yelling, my eyes from crying, my hands from wildly searching my skin, looking for some hope that I just might not have done this thing, again.

AS REALITY AND THE FEAR of being restrained set in quickly, and I knew that baby number ten (3 miscarriages, 6 abortions, 1 Q) was sitting somewhere in a box in pieces, I simmered down enough for my ears to pick up a soft sobbing. I glanced to my left. About two beds down sat a short-haired young woman whom I had noticed earlier in the waiting room. I wasn't wearing my contact lenses, but the blurry image did not hide the familiar cheerless frame.

I remember the boyfriend's monologue. They sat directly outside the check-in area in the seats near the elevators. He sat beside her, his body turned toward her, postured in a reassuring way, locs flowing from beneath his Kangol caressing his gorgeous caramel face (yes, even then, my mind was where it should not have been), lips moving, eyes sensitive. I couldn't hear, but I watched them as she sat with her back straight, clutching her coat, staring solemnly into her lap; not unlike now, only this time, she was slumped over with nothing to clutch, no one in her ear. If she felt anything like me, the boyfriend's prior attempt at consolation and encouragement did nothing for this new moment—when no one is here—when you lie in a room of a dozen or so strangers and the one stranger who would have added some meaning to your life is gone.

I knew before we walked through the metal doors that led to the place where we undressed, donned flimsy gowns and waited some more until one by one we separated into rooms where we would be laid down, intravened, spread, and siphoned of the nuisance that we sought relief from, she did not want any part of this. But I couldn't feel sorry for her then; I was already mentally prepared to rid myself of mine. But now, as I came down from my hysteria, I wondered if her emptiness was anything like mine. I blew my nose into a piece of crumpled tissue that one of the nurses had handed me earlier, and I turned my attention to the blurry slump of tears.

"Are you okay?"

She nodded, keeping her hands and her eyes in her lap. How beautiful was she to respond to my feeble query. Guilt and memory washed over me and I began to tremble. She was me; the person I was when I first ever entered this place five years before. What was I doing? It was almost as if I had been the one to suck the life out of her. We sat in silence and waited until they told us it was okay to get dressed and have beverages and cookies. You need that after you've fasted all night and had your insides scraped.

Someone once reminded me that our beautiful babies are dancing around in unknown glory before our Father. They don't look like chopped meat and they don't remember. This I offer not as license to murder, but as redemption and chance for those who have gone there and don't think that they can ever come back. You can always come home.

It Was April 11, 1999

Journal Entry, June 2008; Regarding April 2009

It was a deep tub. The kind I like, with lion's paws. I filled it as high as I could without drowning; as hot as I could without peeling my skin. I scrubbed. No matter how I prayed, the washcloth was still a washcloth. It was not Brillo. I needed Brillo.

I scrubbed and I cried. I screamed and I hollered and I cried behind a veil of newsprint shower curtains. Personal ads: LOVE WANTED—ANYTHING GOES. I cried while he snored. And I begged God forgiveness. And I asked Him why this had to be. And I cried. And I couldn't stop.

The bath did not remove the stains. She was gone but I still smelled her. It was done but I still lived it. I felt the darkness of where we had been and my chest ached of tears his heart refused to hear. I lay next to him looking for warmth. Peace. Nothing. I listened to him breathe. I listened for something that said, "I didn't mean it and I'm sorry." Something that said, *"even though we did this, we could still be, I can be who you need."*

I did not realize that I would take anything. Just so long as it felt good most of the time and hurt only some of the time and when it hurt some of the time that it didn't hurt too much. I could not name it desperation or faithlessness or futility. And my creation was not what I intended him to be. He could not walk with me.

What was I thinking? How could I not know? I heard the whirring of the vibrator. She was playing. I saw the porn on the screen. She was in the very bed where he would lay me down. At the very same time. How could I not know?

He was there and he was—gentle. Quick. It changed and it was even gentler. I knew it was different. Someone else. But I didn't want to know. He took my hand and placed it on her head. He placed my hand on her head, and I felt her cornrows lead to a perfect bun on top. She was there. I didn't know what to do. I didn't know how to like it.

I'm there. I'm there and I don't know what I'm doing. It's not what I thought. You think things, even though you don't really want them, and I thought that if I ever, I would be good because I know, I know what I want. But it's not what I thought. Not what I want. And it's happening so fast that I can't think. I can't choose. So I'm there, I'm there, and I hear them talking.

"Yo, D, I think she's feelin' it, but I'm not tryin' to have my [. . .] bit off."

She's concerned that I will do damage. But they've already damaged me. Things keep moving—changing places. I'm in an encounter with a nightmare; that malign spirit formerly believed to suffocate or haunt people during sleep.[26] It is living and I am entwined. I will be suffocating and haunted for months. Years. And he will call from time to time to offer me lies.

She's there—under there—her face. She's there and now *I-don't-care*. Something has to come out of this for me. However superficial. However fleeting. However damning. I may die here. I wasn't enough for his release. And even though I could not see, I know this—tonight—this was what he needed. So I let go and my spirit chokes and I don't know if I am alive. Or if I want to be. And she knows. I hold onto the wall. There are noises. My mind is talking, but it's saying so much that I can't nail anything down. I see the reflections—the television flickering shadows on the wall. He has turned the volume down. Or is it that I hear the sounds and he has turned the screen to black? It's an old television. So much noise in my mind. There are shadows.

---

[26] Derived from http://www.merriam-webster.com/dictionary/NIGHTMARES

I have found an ounce of pleasure. The kind that sex partners get when there's no love; when they dump the pent-up; when they're whatever is around at the time. It is the same pleasure I used to get from masturbation. It comes and goes quickly and leaves me feeling dirty and wasted. And she knows. What she feels reveals more than just the flesh that has its way with me.

It is finished. She lies next to me in the dark and watches my peripheral. She sees my eyes that stare at nothing; eyes that wish for one moment to see nothing; eyes that see his shadow to the right of me. I wanted to believe he could love me. I felt as I did when I was twelve-years-old. When my grandfather—my best friend—showed me my true world. On that cold December night, confusion saw its opportunity and rushed in. In the blackness of this cool April-3:00 a.m.; I revisit when I was lost; in this night filled with selfishness and thoughtlessness, I am that little girl again. The one whose last hope was sucked and pulled out by the tongue and fingers of a sixty-five-year-old man. But I am not the little girl who knows how to go numb, anymore. I am the one who is new; who can't visit the places she's just been. I wanted to leave my heart there but I was too much alive.

She tries to comfort me. "It was just an experience . . . even I've never gone this far."

She does not know about the experience that changes who you are and makes these such experiences like death. I was supposed to show her this. She left. He rolled over. *I love you.* I took a bath. It was a deep tub. *I love you and I wanted to share this with you because I love you.* Why does he say this thing that he cannot mean? Why does he want me to believe that this was what I desired? *Just because it wasn't who you wanted doesn't mean it wasn't what you wanted . . .*

On the same night that I was having a sneak-attack ménage a trois, the man of my destiny was marrying a look-alike. Neither of us knew that we were in the wrong beds until he had already said I do . . . until I had already joined my body with another woman . . . until we had invited their demons to cloud over us. It was but a little while; we came to and ran for our lives; but with us came living memoirs of our choices that we would be servant to for many years to come.

Then came September 2003. A friend and I were front and center watching the African American Day Parade go by. An NYC Court Officers float approached. It was led by a small group of uniformed officers. They were step dancing, hard. One of them was rather chubby, but he floated like a feather.

"Wow, that big one can really jump . . . oh my God . . . that's Damon!"

He stopped and pointed as he scanned the crowd. His eyes locked with mine; his finger landed dead between my eyes. But he looked right through me. He kept jumping down the line. And I could feel the nightmare run screaming from my body.

Get Ready

Journal, December 2007, Regarding November/December 1999

Get ready—get ready—get ready, for your change to come; get ready—get ready—get ready, for your change to come . . . [27]

The lyrics of the song pumped loudly through the speakers. As I opened my eyes, they were immediately assaulted by a bright glare from the bulb in the ceiling. Surely, I didn't forget to turn the lights out when I went to bed. Surely, I haven't been asleep for seven hours.

The alarm clock on the CD changer was set to 6:00 a.m. Through my contact lenses (that I was severely warned by my optician not to sleep in) I began to shift my sleepy eyes back and forth between the CD changer and the small dancing figure in front of it. The time was 2:44 a.m. I must be dreaming because I know I set that thing to come on at 6:00 a.m. I climbed out of bed. K, newly three years old, was prancing around in front of the CD changer like a dog on its hind legs. She was stark-naked, grinning from ear to ear. "Get ready, Mommy! Come on, get ready!"

At the time, I couldn't hear, but I discovered later that He was talking to me. Even in my disobedience, He still felt my life was important enough to try to lead me back. So He used my then youngest child, as He often

---

[27] Excerpt from the song *Get Ready* from the gospel group Virtue's 1999 album, also entitled *Get Ready*.

did, to show me that He loved me and didn't care where I'd been. He just wanted me to come home.

But it was three o'clock in the morning. I was tired—tired of life and of me and of K's new obsession with 2:00 a.m. dancing/refrigerator-rummaging/movie fests. I just wanted to sleep for as long as I could. I shooed the dancing K back into her pajamas and bed, where Q lay sleeping peacefully. I turned out the lights and joined them, silently hoping never to awake again.

Why do You love me? I'm worthless. No matter what I do, I can't get this right. Why do You love me? And, if You really love me, why won't You give me what I want?

Hope To Get Over

EVERYDAY IT'S THE SAME. I wake up soaked in guilt, begging for mercy. Hating myself and feeling like a prisoner to something that I should be able to control. I've blamed it on the years. I've blamed it on my blood. I've claimed it as the thorn in my side. It appears I have many thorns. But this one is a killer.

I arise at morning and say, *not today. Today I win.* Daily tasks are riddled with thoughts of a way out; my mind searching for a remedy. I think about extreme measures and I walk in transient confidence; I know that I can cross over.

Then I arrive. It's the place that I come to everyday. There is an aura over that one tiny space—an aura that floats like a beautiful mother; translucent arms outstretched; gray holes for eyes in an opalescent face, offering a welcome smile...*come, sit, there's much to do. No time to plan—we'll take the day as it comes.* I don't know how I forget that she's waiting; I don't know why I always come quietly when I know she wants to kill me.

I have memories of a few times when I had strength. I had will power. Common sense. Someone once told me that chewing gum erodes teeth. I didn't chew gum for years after that. Someone else told me that carbonated water causes acne. So I quit soda. Still another person informed me that unprotected sex could lead to STDs and unwanted pregnancy. I think that's when my Trans-Opal-Mother and I first met. There she was, waiting for me, waving her arms enticingly over a bed or stairwell or backseat of a car like Barbara from The Price Is Right. She would put up with my turn away from gum and soda; but she would not let me pass this by. I lived through two STDs and seven abortions. By now you'd think I'd recognize her. By now, you'd think I'd run away.

And I am so jealous. I am jealous of those who were delivered from addictions instantly. Men and women who professed to give their lives over—God broke the choke hold, just like that. I have never been addicted to drugs or alcohol or gambling. I could claim former sex addiction, but I was never in love with sex; I was just dissatisfied. Dissatisfaction keeps you coming back and trying new things until there's nothing left. But it's all the same. There was a time that I thought I was better than those who struggled with addictions. But the deeper I sink into my fifteen-year pit of dependency on this unreliable source of comfort, energy, strength, the more I realize that it's all the same. But I want out.

It is sugar that I speak of. Chocolate mint, white rice, rich breads, toffees, french fries, pasta. Eating my body. My skin, my hair, my teeth, my loins, my energy, my moods. I know—it all sounds so benign. But there are legless, wheelchair bound people who can attest to it's clutch; and because I lack the obesity or scrawniness that would easily classify me as having an eating disorder, I couldn't get a doctor to pay me any attention.

I have tried to let go on my own. I want to believe that I'm coming to the end. But is the end dying? I mean, real, physical death? My body slowly losing pieces and functions via the ravages of disease that catalyst a chain reaction of anatomic destruction? Will I ever get over? This is not the legacy I want to leave for my children.

It's 9:40AM. I am on my way and I know my Trans-Opal-Mother waits for me. I pray that today, just this one day, I will ignore her offerings. I pray that I hear the voice of The Good Shepherd and follow Him instead . . .

Seven Abortions Part III

From: Quyahni Denise Lewis [mailto: quyahni@yahyah.com]
To: breaktheday@redeemed.com
Date: Mon, 4 Aug 2008 23:09:33
Subject: re:

> . . . I try not to complain about [my period woes] too much these days. I've recently begun to look at it like this: I had seven abortions. That's seven children that never had a chance to grow inside my body; seven sets of contractions that I never experienced; seven womb passages that never took place. I am privileged to spend nearly every day of every month experiencing what feels like pregnancy—everything from contraction-like cramps days before and during my period to morning sickness that makes me wanna hurl—right down to the passing of the blood that is so heavy and so seemingly never ending. I could have killed my babies and had absolutely no connection to them at all. The way I see it, I owe them each nine months of development, an estimated ten hours of labor each, and some blood, sweat, and maybe even tears. So having this crazy period is not a nuisance, although I do wish I wasn't so tired all the time. Even in that, it's a grace that I can't explain. I know I sound crazy; but this is a revelation from God and I appreciate it so much . . . it could be so much worse . . . I could be dead from all those abortions. I could have had my uterus removed and not even seen Quefina, Nia, or Yesenia. But His mercies are not only new every morning; they are far, far beyond anything I could ever deserve . . .

Wisdom of Dawn

To:	quyahni@yahyah.com
Subject:	Re: yeah, I know what you mean . . .
From:	"Dawn" <BreakTheDay@redeemed.com>
Date:	Thu, 22 Jun 2006 09:48:50-0400

I wish you had called me last night. I didn't think you would be up this late. Yahni whenever you are up and maybe can't sleep or you just need to talk . . . please call me. You really are in the eye of the storm. I earnestly feel for you right now.

I just stopped typing and I sat here and thought about what we are both dealing with. I am sitting trying to find words of encouragement to give to you, but it's difficult. I laugh to myself because it seems as if we are both two very wounded soldiers, and it seems as if we are sorta lost out in the midst of the battle field, trying to hold each other up. Before the battle got this deep and heavy . . . we already received our orders from the chief commander . . . that he would come and rescue us when this mission was over, this covert mission that he sent us out on, he didn't tell us why because it was top secret info and even we couldn't know it . . . cause if we did . . . we would mess up the mission's purpose . . . only he knows the "why" . . . and he also told us . . . that all we had to do was go exactly where he told us to go . . . and fight the good fight . . . he told us that no matter what kind of ammunition the enemy would try to come at us with . . . he said to only use the weapons he gave us . . . the standardized weapons that are issued to his soldiers, that can only be activated by those who are truly chosen for this battle, "the few . . . the proud . . . and the brave." He said only use these weapons, do not use any weapon of your own . . . or the ones you might find left behind by the enemy because they will never work . . . he told us.

He said that he was telling us this so that we would not get ourselves killed in this war. He said if we didn't use his weapons . . . we'd get destroyed in the battle . . . and what a shame it would be. Although yes . . . He would carry our bodies out of the war zone, and yes . . . we would still have the right to be buried back at home station where he is . . . cause he promised us that when we first enlisted with him to be in his army, but what a shame to have deviated from the mission when all we had to do was follow his instructions, and not only would we have conquered our enemy, but our chief commander promised us all medals of honor, a huge promotion in rank, and he would even let everybody else see us in our time of glory and honor. So now . . . here we are . . . beat up, I lost my radio transmitter to even be able to call the chief commander . . . I think I know where it might be, but I am pretty much being a coward and don't feel like going to get it because that would take for me to lean on my injuries a little if I move from this spot where you and I are holding our wounds, you still got your communicator, but its transmitting only every now and again, and at this point . . . it sounds like static. We both keep telling one another that we know what we need to do to get to safety, but every time we look out on the actual battle and we see all the bullets flying over our heads . . . more and more . . . back to back pow, pow, pow, pow, pow, pow . . . it seems as if it just doesn't stop. When we see this, it makes us feel so discouraged. It's just like . . . what are we going to do now? And the whole time, our chief commander is able to see our every move from this high-tech equipment he has . . . with a zoom lens, and he's shaking his head looking at us because he knows that he gave us enough training to make it through this battle, he knows our potential to be a mighty force in his army, he wants to give us all the medals and rewards that we want, all we have to do is keep our focus on him (our leader) and we will make it through, just like he said we would. And the sad part about it is that all we really have to keep in mind is how he brought us through the many, many, past battles that we fought in and conquered.

How did we forget?

The ACS Case, Part I

Journal, November 5, 2009; Regarding June 2006-January 2007

I WANTED A LIFE. I believed I didn't have one because people stole it from me. My dreams, unwrapped treasures swathed near-undetectable in martyr syndrome, were still just dreams. I did not know who I was, so I spent a lot of time trying to be something I wasn't fit to be. And I couldn't even tell you what. I liked to believe that I was selfless, but I really was not. That's how I got caught up in an ACS case.

I dread telling this story because I don't want to sound like I'm feeling sorry for myself. I'm done with the pity party. This is about me; about what I did wrong; about how I nearly destroyed my whole family. But I have to share some things that explain how some of my thinking was shaped. Some things that might make others angry. Some things that might hurt. But they need to be told.

Please bear with me while I break it down:

My husband Darius and I had been together nearly six years at the time that all this went down. He had been married twice before and has three sons from his first wife who are all adults, and with whom he didn't have much contact. But Sunshine, his child from his last marriage, was ever present. And, of no fault of hers, attached to her were emotional and spiritual issues that refused to be ignored. Issues that I had to deal with nearly every day.

The home in which we rented a one-bedroom apartment in Queens had been sold, and we had not been able to land an apartment beforehand. We moved away from my best friend Meesha and my very first church home (the people who were closest to me at the time) and, after trying to make it living with friends and relatives, Darius, my two children, Q and K, and I ended up staying in a Harlem homeless shelter for nearly two years. And, while Darius seemed to have many friends and connections, I had to start all over again.

Darius worked two jobs, attended college and worked in ministry and community development. This had been the norm since before we got married. I've been with him through one bachelors and two masters degrees. When his second ex-wife, Teresa, started attending college in 2005, I babysat for her, two nights per week, as well. How I came to accept such arrangements should be pretty plain by the time this story ends.

Darius's and Teresa's marriage had pretty much ended before it began. She was about four months pregnant when Darius left. I heard tell that the relationship was violent. It had come to a head, both their lives were in danger, so Darius thought it best to leave. But that's their story, so that's all I'm gonna say about that.

So along with all the goodies—charisma, a great smile, a strong understanding of the Word of God and a passion for Jesus that overshadowed any idiosyncrasies I could ever harp on—Darius came with some stuff that I could have done without. We both carried luggage into our marriage (I had two babies' daddies before I met my husband; one who was virtually absent, and one whom I wished was). But Darius and I knew we belonged together and were determined to work things out, although we had no idea the fight we were in for.

Sunshine was nine months old when she started hanging out with us. Darius knew that her mother was predictably unpredictable, so he tried to appease her as much as possible; he wanted to keep Sunshine close. Whatever Teresa asked, Darius did. In the beginning, he took Sunshine to every doctor's and WIC[28] appointment and many babysitter

---

[28] WIC stands for Women, Infants and Children. It's a program that provides formula and other nutritional needs for low-income families with pregnant women and children under the age of five.

pickups and drop-offs. This left me—pregnant just two months into our marriage—hurting; often sitting alone in the tiny temporary quarters we shared in a Harlem welfare hotel, watching old VHS tapes and lamenting over my confused life.

Arrangements were often made for me to keep Sunshine for extra days (translation: Teresa asked Darius to babysit, Darius said yes, Darius left Sunshine with me). In addition to the child support that he gave without the typical court battle, whenever she asked, even though we couldn't afford it, he gave Teresa extra money without first discussing it with me. Teresa freely asked favors of me, too. I couldn't stand the woman (and I knew I had no real reason; I was really piqued with Darius for using me, with God for allowing it, and with myself for not knowing my role), but I never declined. I thought it made me look good.

One could easily understand why watching my husband run around like a minion for his ex-wife was just as bad as if he had been cheating.

Darius became the golden calf I fashioned while God was silently at work on the mountaintop inside of me. I pined for his attention, clinging desperately to the hope that he would value me for more than just a help mete. However, my labors were useless; I faded into the background except for when a need arose. I was nothing more than a servant to him, his daughter, and her mother. I was miserable.

It would be forever before this story ended if I told you everything that went on for the first six years. So let me just tell you what went down one Friday evening in the summer of 2006 . . .

JUNE 9 WAS MARKEDLY ONE OF THE WORST EVENINGS OF MY LIFE. I was in the conference room at the church where Darius served as associate pastor. It was evening, after work, and the usual youth stuff was happening in the sanctuary upstairs. I was at my laptop, trying to force out my "life story." Sunshine, who was six and Nia, the third of my four children (one son, three daughters), who was five, were playing in the outer office area where I could see them.

"Put those scissors down! They're dangerous and you know you're not allowed to handle them unsupervised."

I had stepped out of the conference room and found Nia and Sunshine cutting paper. They stopped and I went back to my laptop. Once I was out of sight, the girls went back to playing with the scissors.

I was getting nowhere with my story. I took another break and walked out of the conference room. I looked down at the gray industrial carpet that covered the floors of the conference room, the outer office area, and the surrounding offices. My eyes met a Hansel-and-Gretel trail of six-inch locs. *No! Please tell me they didn't . . .*

They had. Nia had snipped off several locs from the front of her head. There was one small clipping that Sunshine had cut from her own long bushy ponytail, also in the front. The fury came and blinded me; not before I saw the fear in the girls' eyes; but still, it was too late.

I don't even remember from how I a belt ended up in my hand. I was screaming. I grabbed them by the left arm, in turn, swiftly positioned them so that their backs faced me, and delivered six lashes each to their bottoms. Their faces were toward me, their eyes wild with fear that would normally have evoked writhing and running, but in this instance, seemed to have frozen them in place.

I was still screaming, spanking done, when Darius walked in. He told me to calm down, that I was killing myself. I screamed some more . . . at him this time . . . my screaming . . . mixed with the girls' crying . . . I was over the top . . . more than angry . . . not really about the haircutting . . . Sunshine . . . she shouldn't have been there . . . I shouldn't have been responsible for her . . . I was so tired and everything was just wrong.

The screaming took my voice. I went out the next morning—I don't recall where—and met up with Darius and the girls after their gymnastics class. Nia and Sunshine ran to me . . .

"Mommy, you left marks on my leg—"

I cut them off, barely barking with raspy leftover vocals . . .

"I spanked you on your butt, so there wouldn't be any marks on your legs!"

They stared blankly. They didn't respond.

Darius's usually strong and immovable eyes bore disappointment and a sense of trouble to come. My heart knew it was coming, too.

The rest of the weekend was a blur up until Sunday evening, when I was dressing the girls for bed. Purplish blue with red hues was the bruise on Sunshine's right thigh. She had very sensitive skin. Nia's was not so bad; it was noticeable, but less colorful; her skin was darker and less delicate.

I had swung too hard. The belt had found its way around their little bottoms and landed on their thighs. Six times. I could remember my own childhood lashings—extension cords, thick leather belts, mop sticks, even a tree switch once—mostly for things that others did. The agony of any of those instruments landing in the same spot more than once is beggaring description.

I put ice on Sunshine's leg. I thought about calling her mother to explain what had taken place. After all, we were friends, sort of; we were working in collaboration to raise her child. But something in me knew that a phone call would be a waste of time. I could imagine her speaking softly, pretending to be understanding, and assuring me that everything would work out. And then, she would have done exactly what she did the following day.

And I couldn't blame her, really. Teresa hadn't wanted this soap opera any more than I. We were both victims, in a sense. Teresa was just a lot smarter than me; she knew how to use everything to her advantage, even my very mistaken belief that I was the better woman.

And suddenly, all the self-serving reasons why I did all I did for Sunshine, Darius, Teresa, came back to bite me on the butt.

On Monday evening, June 12, 2006, Darius got a phone call from Teresa. She had discovered the bruise. I listened from the living room as Darius talked—he was in our bedroom, way in the back of our four-bedroom apartment. I couldn't make out the words but he was yelling, it was brief, and then there was silence. Darius knew, days before I did, that Teresa had arranged for an investigation by The Agency for Child Services (or, as it's famously known and dreaded in most single-parent and/or low-income households across New York City, ACS). He never told me. But there were things that clued me:

> *Tuesday, June 13, 2006; 11:23 a.m.*
>
> *Sunshine showed up to school just a little while ago[29]. Teresa called early this morning to tell us that she would be late. She came to my office, like she usually does, to give me a hug. I asked Sunshine where she had been. She had been to the doctor. When I asked her what for, she pointed to her right thigh. Teresa had taken her for a tetanus shot. It had begun.*
>
> *1:17 p.m.*
>
> *I just got off the phone with Teresa; I had called to apologize for not calling her and talking to her about the spanking when it first happened; I explained that I didn't mean to hit Sunshine so hard, that I was aiming for her bottom; that it wasn't about the haircutting, but about how hard I worked for the kids and how they just did not seem to respect or listen to me; that I was just so tired and no one seemed to care. I was trying to be humble, but I couldn't manage directly apologizing for the spanking itself. I felt justified for my actions, conceding only to the fact that I shouldn't have administered the punishment while I was angry.*
>
> *Teresa responded with her usual spurious humility and gentleness. She said that she understood my struggles and that she wanted to help with my overflowing plate of maternal responsibility. She said that she knew I did not mean to hurt Sunshine, but she preferred that that type of punishment be given out by her and Darius only. She also told me that she had to "do what she needed to do to cover herself, to make sure that she didn't get in trouble." I never even asked her what she meant. But I knew. I was just hoping beyond all hope that she hadn't done what I knew she had . . .*

---

[29] Sunshine attended Kindergarten at the school where I worked

I found out officially at one of the kids' performances that following Friday.

Teresa was in the lobby area of the kids' after-school program when I walked in. I hugged her, but it was fake, and I was unhappy with myself because of it. When the performance was over and we were all sitting around eating, I went to her and asked for a second hug, and forgiveness, once more.

"Don't mind me," I whispered through tears that would not obey my silent pleas to cease. "I'm just tired . . . I'm just so tired . . . "

"I know," she said, "I know . . ."

Teresa was surrounded by her own people at that moment: her sons and their girlfriends, her first ex-husband and Sunshine. But she turned her attention away from the laughter she was enjoying with them to receive my embrace. We held each other tight and long; then she took me by the hand and led me away from the small groups of people. She killed me softly as she spoke . . .

"I just wanted to warn you that, when I took Sunshine to the doctor's office the other day, he reported the bruise to ACS. But I want you to know that I am with you and we're going to get through this as a family. I know what it's like to have someone I love taken away from me. (She was talking about when she was on crack and her children were removed from her home.) I love you and we'll get through this together."

Teresa was still holding my hand, looking into my eyes. I remained gazing into hers, too . . . disappearing behind them . . . nervous smile frozen to my face . . . it was not pain that I felt . . . not yet . . . I was melting . . . or . . . peeling . . . dissolving . . . into nothing. I knew my life was over.

I didn't know what to do. I told Darius about my conversation with Teresa when we got home that night. He smiled, kissed me on the forehead, and said something similar to what Teresa had said . . . something about *getting through it together*. He still had not told me that he knew about it already, that he had already heard from ACS, and that we had an appointment for the following week. He called me at work the day before to let me know.

THE VISIT TO ACS WAS TERRIFYING. The last time I had been at that office, I was a seventeen-year-old foster child and the agency was on my side. This time, when I entered, I felt like I did when I was ten years old, on a roof with a knife to my throat, being led behind a door in the purple night, staring at death. Only this time the knife was photos of Sunshine's bruised thigh in the ACS worker's hand, threatening to cut deep and lead me into a darkness that might very well take my life. This time, it was my fault that I was about to be probed by a stranger. Just days before, I was everybody's hero. Now, I was the worst kind of offender: I was an abuser.

The ACS worker (henceforth referred to as Ms. ACS) was a hefty Black woman with raccoon eyes (from too much rubbing, probably; no doubt she was a severe allergy sufferer), smoker's lips, and a threatening glare. She ran through the ACS spiel, complete with all the necessary warnings; made mention of having spoken with Darius days after the incident, as soon as Sunshine's doctor had contacted ACS (my trust of my husband was slowly diminishing; why would he not want me to be prepared for this?). She began her questioning, which included some points from her interview with Sunshine and Teresa:

June 21, 2006; 9:17 p.m.

We went to the ACS appointment today. I found out that Sunshine had told them that she is afraid of me. I looked surprised when I said to Ms. ACS, "Afraid of me? Really? The same little girl that tells her teacher that she has to use the bathroom half a dozen times a day just so she can come to my office and give me a kiss and a hug? Hmmph!"

I know it's true; I'm not exactly nice to her; I do not hide my resentment from her and whenever Darius has something to say about it, I blast him and point to all the tangible things I do for Sunshine. I mention the counterfeit embraces, smiles, and praise I give her that are not really for her, but for me; for when I need to prove that I'm a good stepmother.

I've been a bully to Sunshine and, in this interview, my bully's heart was open to the elements of Ms. ACS's threatening stare and convicting tone. I was vulnerable and close to reliving the panic attacks I suffered from 2001-2003. How I wished I could turn back the clock, not back to the spanking, back about six years, when I first met my husband. Things would have been different, I think.

Ms. ACS asked if my relationship with Darius came about via infidelity, if I had interfered with his marriage to Teresa. Teresa once—no, twice—accused me of conceiving Nia while they were still together. I remember her exact words the first time she said it during a 1:47-a.m. phone call: "You conceived that child during my marriage to Darius!" I never got a word in edgewise; she was railing on me over some comments I made about a lie she had been keeping up to get more money from my husband . . .

I was trying to figure out what planet she was on. Sunshine is a year and three months older than Nia; in order for Darius and me to have conceived Nia while he was still with Teresa, I would have had to have carried Nia from August of 1999 until May of 2001. I may be a little chubby, but I'm no elephant . . . I can barely hold a child in me for nine months, let alone two years . . .

I knew nothing of their relationship before Darius and I came together. I didn't even know them by name. They were strangers to me—they began attending the same church as me nearly two years after I had joined and we were never introduced. I left the church for seven months (I was struggling with my own relationship problems) and when I returned, Darius and Teresa had been married, pregnant with Sunshine, and separated all in a matter of five months. Darius and I began courting four months after their separation and were married two months after their divorce.

I bet Teresa didn't tell Ms. ACS that I spent five years bringing up Sunshine alongside my own babies. On paper, she lived with her mother, but she spent most of her time in my home. I did whatever her parents asked and then some. I took care of her while they finished college, even though I was dying to get my own degree. I gave Sunshine everything that I gave my own kids.

She was often feverish, nauseous, and had diarrhea in her toddler years, and was dropped off to me in that condition—a lot. Darius and I weren't sure what to attribute it to—didn't know if she was contagious—we just received her and, while Darius went to his overnight job or to school or to church or some other meeting or function, I sat up in the threes and fours of the mornings nursing Sunshine's sour stomach, making visits to Harlem corner stores at the crackhead hour for over-the-counter remedies, cleaning vomit and diarrhea, administering rounds of cool baths and alcohol/vapor rubs to break stubborn fevers, running through all of Nia's Pull-Ups and baby wipes at a time when we could barely afford food.

I went into that ACS interview not knowing how to speak anymore. I am a writer, a poet, a singer. My normal near-perfect articulation and eloquence were reduced to the sputtering of unnecessary information that I was sure made me look and sound asinine. Darius sat quietly to my right, listening, almost wincing, awaiting his turn to speak, no doubt silently praying or trying to telepath *"Shut up, Stupid!"* from his brain to mine as I rambled off answers to each question.

Ms. ACS let us know that she "did not like what [she] saw" in the photos of Sunshine's thigh and that normally, in cases where bruising was present, indication was inevitable.

An indication would mean that I would be listed "in the system" as a child abuser until my youngest child, Yesenia, who was then only one and a half, was twenty-eight years of age. If I ever applied for a position having anything to do with children, the hiring agency would find out this information in a background check. Most agencies that have the best interest of children in mind wouldn't even look at me twice. I was an admin at a new charter school and, thankfully, my bosses assured me that they had no intentions of firing me. Yet I ran the risk of acquiring a twenty-eight-year scar for causing a bruise that had already faded. But I never considered the years of bruising of Sunshine's heart.

Darius felt he needed to coach me on how to "be" during this ordeal. I wonder what it is inside of a man that makes him say stuff that he should know—after having messed up so many times before—is going to get him told off, punched out, or dumped. I wanted him to shut up and leave me alone. There were days when I wanted him to go away. He had no idea what was happening inside of me, what I lived with every day; every moment obsessed over hours before it is born, every millisecond replete with fear. I felt so alone, as I had so many times during my life, as I had during the first years of our marriage, as I would be so many times in my future with him.

I DON'T MEAN TO TELL THE STORY THIS WAY; I don't mean to make my husband and his ex-wife sound like villians. But I can only share what it looked like to me; what it felt like to me. They seemed to be playing me, using me.

During the first six months of 2005, I had developed a bond with Teresa that was really strange; she and I would talk on the phone every day for hours, like best friends. I shared things with her that I probably shouldn't have; we had gotten that close. I never really laid down my guard, never really trusted her, but I couldn't let go of the relationship; I was determined to push past my apprehensions and make whatever "it" was work.

She would drop off my daughter K to school in the mornings, we included each other in family and church functions—my kids even spent the night at her house a couple of times. We were definitely living in the Twilight Zone; but I thought I was being a good Christian. I thought it was something that God wanted and—no matter how uncomfortable it was—my duty to fulfill. I don't know what Teresa was thinking, but Darius was a happy camper; his "two women" were getting along, which meant no challenges for him.

And now, Teresa was chillin' waiting for the ACS gavel to come down on me, waiting for the scarlet letter ("A" for "Abuser") on my chest, and Darius would only have to hang around and be the supportive, comforting husband and be back in my good graces once the smoke cleared, ready to put some more stuff on me that wasn't mine to carry. Things would be back to normal for them.

But was this the end for me? Would my children be taken away from me? Would everyone, everywhere, think that I was a child abuser?

What I Wanted to Say

i have written you many letters. some of love. some of hate. mostly hate. i have told you what i think of your lies. lies that broke my very soul. lies that tore into me and snatched the remaining pieces of my heart. snatched my identity bald. i have called you invisible things. some with capital *b*s. some with capital *f*s. some with capital *ho*s. i have used them to carve your face into unidentifiable pieces. i have cut those pieces into finer un-re-connectible ones. i have scalped and gutted you—ripped you—i have killed you over and over and over again.

i have wallowed in the excrement of unforgiving you. for years. and loving you. while i hate you. hating me for hating loving you—loving hating you.

and as i rebuild and trudge on with my artificially induced joy, i know that there are those that wrote me letters just the same. called me invisible bs and fs and hos. carved me and scalped me and . . . well . . . you know. the repeated murder of self—the spiritual suicide attempts to exhaust himself . . . herself of every single thought/feel/smell of me.

still i don't want to share the same air with you. but i'll be careful what i wish for.

it will come that i set you free and live all of me. it will come . . . it will come . . . it will come . . .

. . . strangely enough, your murder of me brought me new life. i should thank you for that. i did not do so in my murder[30] of you. i hope you will forgive me.

---

[30] assassination of character

The ACS Case, Part II

Journal Entry, November 8, 2009; Regarding June 2006-January 2007

I HAD SOME FRIENDS WHO WORKED WITH THE AGENCY. None of them could make the case go away, but one of them looked up the file for me and found out that Teresa had actually called the police. Teresa had been arrested for assault a few years prior—something about a love triangle gone wrong. It seemed as if she wanted me to experience all she had been through—the removal of her children, central booking—everything. But the police had told Teresa to take Sunshine to the doctor, instead, because they knew that the doctors were mandated to report what they saw.

There were so many painful and embarrassing parts to the investigation. I had to inform the fathers of my first two children that they would be getting a call from ACS. Q's dad laughed at the thought of anyone thinking I was an abuser. Our relationship had been rocky and crazy when we were together; we were young, we made a lot of mistakes, but he knew enough to know that I didn't want to physically hurt a child.

K's dad, however, was far from my number one fan. I listened over the phone to a tornado of familiar degrading and condescending verbiage. Even though it was no longer a regular part of my life, as it had been when we were together, it still had the same effect.

And I could share this torment with no one. Overwhelming angst took my strength. I watched my children live and laugh and play and I worried that my pain would seep into their little hearts and interrupt their childhood; yet I could not get myself out from under the sadness. On top of all that, because Darius thought it made me look good if I still cared for Sunshine regularly, because he thought that it was what the Lord would want me to do, I still had to look Sunshine in her face nearly every day while I awaited my fate, while Darius and Teresa continued with business as usual, while I pushed further away from life and deeper into hopelessness.

My prayers were woeful . . . desperate and full of doubt. I had forgotten every promise God had ever made me; the scriptures seemed to speak of hope for others and none for me.

My days were consumed with all kinds of crazy, but mostly with thoughts of my stepdaughter's mother. I wanted to believe that Teresa was a good person at the same time that I wanted to believe she was bad.

FROM THE VERY BEGINNING OF OUR RELATIONSHIP, I felt a connection to Teresa, although I chose to focus on all the off-putting things I learned about Teresa from my husband. It was my choice to accept his depiction of her (and, don't get me wrong, she definitely gave me reason not to trust her, but); I had my own mind and harping on Teresa's negatives made me feel good about myself. I never gave myself time to see the good stuff that was no doubt buried underneath the ugly I painted her to be.

But there was empathy, a familiarity that made me mindful of Teresa against my will. Even though I vacillated between caring for, and loathing, her, I sensed an attachment that I could not elucidate.

Once, in an e-mail exchange we had when Teresa and I were in the third year of our distorted friendship, Teresa referred to Darius as our "shared husband." As freaky and twisted as that sounded, our relationship really was like one of a modern-day harem; we were like Darius's concubines without the sharing of the marriage bed. But this revelation would come later.

And Teresa was everywhere I was, it seemed, which made it difficult for me to manage capitulating to my own offenses. It was like being awake in a recurring nightmare.

This is how it was about a week after the abuse case began. We were following our normal routine; I kept Sunshine on Tuesdays and Thursdays, in addition to every weekend, while Teresa attended classes. It was the Tuesday after she broke the news of the impending case. She had called me at work because she wanted to drop off some things for Sunshine. She sounded sad. I assured her that all was well, even though it was.

"Of course, you can drop her things off, you know it's never a problem . . ."

When she arrived, solemn-faced, at my office door, I thought I saw remorse in her eyes for real, this time, like maybe she regretted pushing the ACS button. I believed her sorrow; I wanted to embrace her and tell her that I loved her, to say sorry over and over again and just believe that we could still salvage whatever our relationship was in spite of what it had become.

I had seen and heard Teresa cry in the past and had not once been moved, although I often pretended to be. (I have never met anyone who could make the water flow like she could; I envied her for this.) But on this day . . . *she did have a heart,* I thought. It just always seemed to be masked by double-talk and deception, no yield to the act of loving purely. This type of heart was usually formed by the lingering pain of a childhood interrupted, a distrust that could teach one to *be* untrustworthy. I knew it well because I was the same.

As the days went on, I was more and more broken, yet I still did not put my foot down. I told Darius, but not Teresa, that I needed some space and really didn't want to be responsible for Sunshine anymore. This argument always ended with me caving to keeping things as they were, which made me loathe the three of them even more.

And even though I had no right, I blamed them for the trouble I was in. It was not their fault that I thought it was okay to spank Sunshine, that I didn't draw lines. Shouldn't I have known how to conduct myself in this? Did no one tell me before I began? Was I informed, but just not listening?

> *July 16, 2006; 2:47 p.m.*
>
> *My friend Nikia has been a huge comfort to me. She had been through an ACS case—a false accusation—and survived without an indication. Nikia is loving, but firm with me; she won't allow me to play the victim. She is forcing me to see all the condemnation and judgment that I had hidden in my heart against Sunshine and Teresa. I knew it was there, I just didn't want to own it, but Nikia is having none of that.*
>
> *She cuts into the places that I won't venture. She cries sometimes when she has to tell me the truth about myself because she knows that my response will most likely be anger—that I will lash out at her before accepting what I have become. I can't lie, I despised her for it, at first, but I am quickly coming to appreciate her willingness to be vulnerable, to be my sounding board, to expose me so that I can be free.*

The summer was long. I spent it often in my accuser's company. We did not commune and exchange pleasantries, but we were at the same venues, watching our children perform or awaiting the usual drop-off or pickup of Sunshine. By this time, I had stopped communicating with Teresa. I didn't understand how she could leave her child with someone who wouldn't even speak to her. And Ms. ACS didn't seem to find it odd that, even though I was being cited for abuse, Sunshine continued to spend most of her time with me.

On some of those long summer nights, I had dreams about Teresa:

> *July 21, 2006*
>
> *Last night I dreamt that I was at work and Teresa was there, following me around and talking incessantly. She was dressed all in black—a micro-mini leather skirt with ruffles, midriff, fishnet stockings, and pumps. Her hair was a giant Bozo the Clown orangey-red gelled mass, sitting atop her head like a Mohawk minus*

> the shaved sides. Her face was plastered with makeup. People came and went, annoyed as I tried to explain Teresa's behavior, never once looking at Teresa, conducting their business with me, and leaving while Teresa continued her endless monologue.

July 31, 2006

> I had another weird dream last night. I was with all of my children in a familiar neighborhood, and there was a woman—a small woman, about 5 feet tall—whose child had tripped and fallen. I tried to help the child, and the woman gave me a look that let me know that she didn't want my help, but I continued to help anyway, and even asked Quentin to help, who was very reluctant to do so.
>
> By the time that dream ended, the woman was wearing an evil smirk that read, "I'll teach you to stick your nose where it doesn't belong." I asked her for a ride to where ever we were going. We all got into her car (it was very overcrowded) and she drove us to a place reminiscent of my past, where there were crowds of confused people, some standing like sentinels with mean faces, some inebriated and raucous. There were several barbecue grills fired up in places that they didn't belong and noise and chaos and obstacles were everywhere we turned. Someone on a loud speaker somewhere was trying to convince me to jump off a ledge . . .

The dreams bled the haunting truth of the backfiring of my secret hope for Teresa's demise . . .

But it didn't have to be that way. I was never obligated to befriend Teresa. I would not have been so competitive had I not done so. The birthday parties we planned together, the Thanksgivings at my house that Teresa invited herself to, everything about our relationship was so unnatural, so uncomfortable; and yet I continued in it for a long time. I should never have bought into the idea that this was how it was supposed to be.

August 1, 2006

> The truth is, I'm afraid of her. Why am I so afraid of her? Oh, I hate that I'm afraid of her . . .

I'm afraid of what she represents, I guess. She seems so sure of herself. She has so much influence. She seems able to get everyone—even my husband, to whom she's supposedly a bad taste in the mouth—to jump through hoops for her. I have never been able to get anyone to do that for me. Yet all she has to do is tell a sob story or come up with some scheme and she's got people ready to do her bidding. Everywhere she goes. Of this, I'm afraid.

And the more I fear her, the meaner I am to her, and to Sunshine. And I know she knows it. She doesn't respond to my sniping voice or sneering eyes. She knows she's got me by the throat, and I know it too, so why don't I just stop? Why am I giving her ammo?

There's no love in me . . . there can't be . . . cuz there's no fear in love . . .[31]

---

[31] 1 John 4:18

2006

My heart was broken in 2006; not by a thing that was done to me, but a thing that was done for me. Truth be told, I broke my own heart; truth be told, I saw myself inside of another. I did not want to see; I tried to separate realities, but there is only one.

There is a reminder; it is with me every day. A fragility that I would do without, but some part of me is glad it's here; this kind of broken heart can only be renewed, not repaired. Repair implies putting a couple of pieces back together again; this kind of broken heart; this is flesh that was torn to pieces. A lioness upon her catch barely leaves skin and bones; there wasn't much left of me.

Truth be told, it began long ago; truth be told, I would say 1969. The devil paid a visit; the lord suggested me, why would he play such a game? The question then became, why am I worthy? I would soon find it to be glory for my head.

So while I was devouring my own heart and becoming what I hate; becoming what I feared; fear made me a predator. I preyed to fill a void unfillable by my prey; I had to look at me in the mirror; it was hard not to wretch.

So back to my broken heart, my shredded-meat-heart; this kind of broken heart has casualties. It explodes and consumes those around it; it floods and drowns the ones who would throw you a life raft. It erupts and turns everything to ashes.

Oh, what a friend we have in Jesus. I used to get annoyed by that song because it was everywhere I went; too cliché-ish; too overdone; but now I know that my tartar heart would be hanging out of my chest as I reached through the bars; flesh burning and resetting; burning and resetting; begging for a vapor—any condensation, anything.

There is no tomorrow; and living on borrowed breath is not consolation but a welcome memoir. I will use it as best I can; I will use it as often as I can. I will live in the redemption of when I gave that chewed-up-heart over. I will pace myself while the healing comes; I will pace myself while the healing connects; I will pace myself while the healing revives the casualties, brings up the drowned, arises up from the ashes.

This is peace. This is finally a real person, knowing misgivings wait at every bend, but no longer trusting in human abilities to be free. My heart was broken over the course of time; my new heart shares and makes whole.

The ACS Case, Part III

ON THE ADVICE OF ANOTHER CLOSE FRIEND who was in the middle of a similar battle, I gathered written character references from my employers, coworkers, ministry partners, and friends. I wanted to prove to ACS that I wasn't who those bruises said I was; I was a woman learning; I didn't know the rules until now.

Ms. ACS had sixty days to finalize the case. She didn't have to use all sixty days, but she did. She visited our home on the very last day to check our refrigerator, interview the children, see where they slept and make sure they were okay. *Then she said it.* I had been indicated. She said that I would soon receive the notification in the mail. She informed me that I had ninety days to appeal, but made sure to tell me that none of her indications had ever been overturned.

I glanced at Darius, who was nervously asking Ms. ACS questions. Hatred beyond anything I had ever known rose up from my belly and burned like vomit in my esophagus. I hated Teresa, hated Sunshine. But in that moment, I hated Darius most of all. He knew from the beginning what kind of drama his ex-wife could bring. But instead of protecting me, he brought it into our home. And in it—because of it—I had left myself open to spoil.

The ensuing melancholy devoured me. Ms. ACS left, Darius tried to talk to me about appealing, I set him on fire with venomous expressions. I stormed to the back of our apartment and locked myself in my sanctuary—the bathroom—the only place where I could shut the door and find a few moments of peace. I fell to my knees before my altar—the edge of the bathtub—crying and howling until my head hurt—blinded by tears and hoarse from helpless bellowing. I called Nikia and listened to her prayers while I howled away the rest of my voice, until my headache became a migraine that threatened to invoke vomiting, until I was completely dry.

I cut Sunshine off. I would no longer babysit. Darius had Teresa discharge her from the school where I worked, and she could no longer stay extra days during the week. When she visited, all the responsibility for her care was solely on Darius.

If Sunshine had been treated differently than my own children it was magnified now. She couldn't be a regular kid around me (not that she ever could before)—couldn't have a squabble with her half and stepsiblings without getting a totally uncalled-for earful. She was only six years old and, for more than five of those years, she had been in the midst of an adult battle. Her innocence and peace sacrificed and overshadowed by our ignorance. She was blameless, but I made her guilty. I didn't see a child. I only saw Teresa, Darius, my indication letter.

I wanted to start over again minus everyone, except the children I gave birth to. But I had nowhere to go.

I spent the next two and a half months—almost the entire ninety-day appeal window—swimming in bitterness and almost missed my opportunity to dispute the indication. I had given up. But Darius, who I was slowly letting back in, convinced me to try. So I sent the letters of reference, wrote a history of my care of Sunshine, poured out my bleeding heart and waited.

My appeal was denied, but I received a copy of the official report; and I found errors therein. Darius had been accused of being present during the spanking. That wasn't true; he had shown up shortly afterward. The report said that I had inflicted lacerations—open wounds—on Sunshine. There were no lacerations. I wrote to the Office of Appeals once more, no longer asking for a reversal or a fair hearing, but only for them to correct the mistakes.

That was early November 2006. I had heard nothing more from them and continued with the repair of what was left of my life. Darius and I went to counseling. Much of me wanted to leave him, but the part of me that loved him and knew that he had been temporarily blinded by man's natural inclination to fix things was willing to yield to his appeal for couples' therapy. The sessions went well and, as I began to heal, I longed to be free of the odium I harbored toward Teresa and Sunshine. I could no longer hold them prisoner to my transgressions.

THEN, ONE EVENING, IN JANUARY OF 2007, I went into my sanctuary, again, and put my heart on the altar.

"Lord, I don't want to hate anymore. This is nasty and I don't like it, I don't want it on me. Please take this thing from me. I want to love."

The next night, I came home from a meeting with our head pastor's wife about resuming the women's ministry that I had stepped away from when all the ACS drama began. It was a good meeting; we had solid plans and were excited about getting the ball rolling. But it was the end of a long work day and I just wanted to get home and rest.

When I arrived at our apartment, I immediately went to my sanctuary again, looking for some peace, when Darius opened the door. I was annoyed with him for a reason I don't remember. But he had a smile on his face that was reminiscent of our courtship that softened my heart a little.

"I don't usually open your mail," he said, "but, this time, I'm glad I did."

He handed me a large manila envelope. In it was a one-page letter that said:

> *Your request to have the above-referenced report of maltreatment amended to unfounded and sealed has been referred to the Bureau of Special Hearings ("Bureau") to be scheduled for a hearing. However, please be advised that the Administration for Children's Services has advised the Bureau that it would not oppose the relief you are seeking. Accordingly, the above-referenced report will be amended to unfounded and sealed by the New York State Central Register. Given that the relief you have sought has been granted, you will*

not need to appear for a hearing, and this letter will serve as a final decision on the matter . . .

As I laughed in disbelief, I remembered another dream; one that occurred a year before the ACS drama began:

April 2005

> . . . *I was very pregnant and I was standing on a corner near a row of brownstones. There was a large tour bus turning the corner. As it turned, it began to tip over in my direction. "I knew this would happen one day," I said to myself. As the bus tipped, I moved closer to the buildings that were lined up along the block I was on. The bus fell against the building and began to slide down; and I got on my hands and knees and prepared to be crushed.*
>
> *But as the bus came down, it began to rise up from the bottom—it was levitating on its side! I heard my husband calling my name . . . "She's not answering me, but I know she's not dead!" he said.*
>
> *I crawled out from under the bus. I ran to Darius and grabbed him by his collar and pulled him toward me. "The kids! Where are the kids?" I asked this question even though I knew they were fine. "They're inside," he said.*
>
> *I went inside of one of the brownstones. There were wall-to-wall people on the ground floor, from the entrance to the small living room where they formed a circle. In the circle were three men wrestling with a woman. They were trying to help her, but she was fighting them.*
>
> *The woman broke away from them and spun in my direction. She raised her hand to hit me and stopped in midair. She looked at me, and then turned around and continued wrestling with the three people in the circle. They wrestled her to the floor and the dream ended . . .*

I read the letter over and over again. The room that had served as my crying chambers five months prior became the place where my face washed with tears of joy, where I found my love again.

But all of this was marked by a *necessary* unrest—a knowing that would gnaw at me for years—that made me think about the favor I had been given; it keeps me in check. Some trauma remains (high blood pressure, heart damage, and PTSD); icing on the cake of a very hard life, and yet they aren't sentence enough. I was glad to have had my name cleared. *But my God, my god, I didn't deserve such mercy!* Still, along with repercussions cloaked in grace, I accepted my own forgiveness.

By spring of 2007, I had allowed Sunshine into my heart again:

May 20, 2007; 4:00 p.m.

> *Sunshine woke up yesterday morning with a pain in her neck. She told me first, and I sent her to Darius. Even though my heart was slowly softening and I missed sharing my love with her, I was determined to stick to the new arrangements—Darius would take care of his child, and I would take care of mine.*
>
> *But this morning, when I went to the bathroom where Sunshine was showering to hurry her along, I opened the door to a rosy, pudgy little face and smoky brown eyes filled with tears.*
>
> *"Is your neck still hurting?"*
>
> *Sunshine replied, "yes," stifled sobs choking her response. I wrapped her in her robe and took her to the kids' bedroom, laid her down upon the pink futon mattress that was folded in half on the floor by the bedroom door. I went to the kitchen and made her a Ziploc ice pack and took it back to the bedroom where she lay silently, tearfully. I sat down next to her, rested her head on my chest, gently put the ice pack on the right side of her neck and rested my chin upon her head.*

I held the pack there and the two of us sat quietly for a long while. Normally, a child wouldn't keep still with an ice pack on her neck because it usually burns before it numbs the pain away. But Sunshine fell asleep. She was probably so exhausted from the ache that she didn't care, or she was suffering silently like she always does. We were going to be late to church, but I didn't care. There were sighs from both of us, each exhale releasing years of stifled breath, my heart melting faster than the ice in the Ziploc bag on Sunshine's neck, thousands of hours of undue heartache leaving . . . I could feel her peace return . . . she is so beautiful . . . she did not deserve such pain . . .

SUNSHINE'S NECK WAS BETTER, finally; my spirit was, too. I was leery, still, because there were things unfinished and miles to go, but I embraced Sunshine moment by moment and did her no harm ever again.

The following spring, I called Teresa. It was a brief but good talk; there were tears and there was release. I learned that I did not have to place my trust in, or commune with, my husband's ex-wife. But I would treat her well. And I would let her be Sunshine's mother.

No longer preoccupied with speculation, I yielded to the freedom process. I reacquainted myself with the delight of my own children that I had traded for clouds of bitterness.

I know that my good intentions will often be met with resurfacing old memories and the enticement to disparage and condemn again. But I no longer lay down arms to such reasoning; I continue to press forward as more facets of my unique family are uncovered. And I have accepted the new way of things. I have finally found my place.

From Shoni

On Wed, Nov 12, 2008 at 3:48 p.m., T <shoni@savedforreal.com> wrote:

Hey . . . It's crazy right now. *Everybody* is going through some stuff unlike stuff before, but trust that you're gonna come out as pure gold. *Envision a fabulous new gown*, long and flowing and unlike anything you've ever seen. You want that gown, girl, because nobody else has it, and it's made just for you, Yahni. It was tailor-made specific to your measurements. You *know* you're gonna be *fierce* in that gown. *And the shoes*! I can't even describe them, but you know the ones that go with that gown. Well, picture that gown and those shoes are made of pure gold! *Pure gold* that can be worn lavishly. The only thing you have to do to get that perfect outfit that makes your boobs sit up and behave and melt your gut away *completely* is *praise and worship*. That's it! *Praise and worship* are the price you must pay for what you want. Don't look at any of the stuff that is taking your focus off that golden dress and dem nasty shoes. *Nothing*! Look to Him who spun that gown and cobbled those shoes for his princess (uh . . . that's *you*). Who in hell can take that away from you? Who is worth *that*? Bless them and keep on moving! Don't sweat that stuff, Yahni. You *must* have that gown and those shoes because when you and me and Charmin step out . . . you can't be lookin' a hot mess because I'ma be mad that you didn't get your gown together. Mine is gonna be *sick* and you know my shoes are like 4 1/2 inches. Hair, nails, face . . . *flawless*! Get it, Miss Thing! Get your praise and worship on *hard*! And get that ensemble! We got a party to go to for *eternity*, woman!

Chapter 2—Poetry

Let Me Write

Let me write
Let me dress up blue and white with words that dance across the pain I used to love
Let me loose so I can steal away the torment of many who wear the shoes I used to fit
Let me give my heart now empty of remorse and regret to be filled with burdens that you will carry
Let me write

Let me write
Let me cry bark and leaves and roots of trees; organic tears to cure the spells that bind the hearts that knew no better
Let me spare the weak and free the passionate and enlighten the sleeping and awaken the dead
Let me write

Let me write
Let me bleed love that rescued me; love that closed the wounds; love that broke the albatross that choked life and hung my head
Let me paradigm the second womb passage; the adoption that came at a thick burgundy red price
Let me be the memoir to grace that carries; mercy that perpetuates; the song that sings forever
Let me write

Let me write
Let me, because I have joy and strength and peace when bodies drop and tears burn eyes red and minds depress brows furrowed and flesh betrays loins guilty and hearts give up beating
Let me be full and fill up and fill in and fill out; giving no place to turn back; no hole to fall into; no stains; no smudges; no trace of what it was
Let me write

Let me write
Write for the broken; write for the unspoken; write for the blind; write for the unfound; write for the one that is not yet one
Let me write because mothers sometimes leave when fathers do; because there are generations that are dying to be free; dying
Let me write

Let me write
Give me back my brothers and my sisters who lend themselves to abuse to be loved by bruises and diseases and fake highs that erode esteem and sit heavily on backs and heads and arms and feet
Let me run into the prisons wielding the keys; let me write let me write let me write because I know
I know the song will change
Let me write

Let me write
Let me be the
It is finished
To the
Please keep cutting me down;
The
I am invaluable
To the
Make me feel worthless, please;
The
I don't need you more than love
To the
I won't be without you
so I'll just be with you
Without your love;
The
I want to live
To the
Please kill me now

Let me write it down; write it off; write it in; write it away and write it away and write it away and write it away . . .

Let me write

Let me write and I will open the windows and I will let it fly over and over again and it will clean the dirty air and it will fall in the middle of the drug exchange; fall; in the middle of the sharing of AIDS; fall; in the middle of the gang initiation; fall; in the middle of the teasing of the one who doesn't fit in; fall; in the middle of the bullying; fall; in the middle of the touching them wrong; fall; in the middle . . . let—me—write . . .

Let me write

Let me write and it will not be about me; let me and there will be fruit; let me write and I will write it away . . . and I will write it away . . . I will write it away . . . write it away . . . away . . . peace . . .

Skin Deep

Beauty/physical/a temporary thing/peel back the skin and hear me sing/ naked/I come to you/O, pray, will you see?/beyond the mounds/the curves/ the flesh that seem to be/where lies the extent of most human desire/no bother to seek the inner/the higher/I offer the spiritual/to those who sleep/ to awaken you to the true beauty/skin deep.

He Made Me

She laid her life on his bed
Across a linty, knitted bedspread
Cotton sheets, dingy from lovers before
She opened and in came the breath of life

Her betrothed
Breathin' heavy cuz the work
He be workin' hard
She heavy breathin' sighs from the push of another
Above her

The wedding
The bells
The altar spoiled with lies
The kiss that sealed the fate
Her belly swellin' with the next lie she gon' tell

Borinquen Daddy
El no quiere bambina, mami
Tiene una familia
Adios
A dios

A yella chile
A yella chile
Who he knew she wasn't his
But he loved her anyway
They took her papa chocolate
In the blackness of the day

Generational things
She needed to be her
She needed to be someone
She needed to be free
They had to steal some things from her to make it

Borinquen daddy
If she could know his name
To touch the side she doesn't know
She could dream again

The loneliness she smiled away
The tears she couldn't cry
Snatched her once upon a time in nineteen eighty-five
She conquered with her flesh, you know

Things ain't always how they look
La niñita esta una estrella
I see her even on rainy nights
And her Borinquen daddy
He taught her how to shine.

Holding On
December 1996

The song was for you
You are all I hear when I hear it
All I hear
Is you

The song was from me
But me, you don't see
When they play it
I don't come to you

I know you taste her memory
Like yesterday, when you're tasting me
Vividly, on your tongue, she, the one who got away

Don't I want to take her place?
No, but I'd surely like to erase her face
I hope you plan to keep me for at least another day.

The poem I write for you
It flows from where you are
In me
In me—it flows from there

The poem to you, from me
But the lyrics, they don't reach
Can't find you
Anywhere

You're not seeing the words in your head
Maybe you wish it were she instead
In the black and white, the one who got away?

But it's me in the paper—me in the ink
And although it may be of her you think
I hope you plan to keep me for at least another day.

It's creepin' upon me
Rather steadily
The day I pray not
To come to be

You won't even have to say
I know
I'll know it
Anyway

Please don't tell me if it's she
And don't you tell her that it's me
Guess that she is not the one who really got away

Well, at least I've got my dignity
Cuz I know it's far too late for me
To hope you plan to keep me for at least another day

Don't say, don't say
Just pause, just glance
The words through almond eyes will dance
Actually, I'd rather you just go

Although I may end up
Losing the fight
I know that I did something right with you
I know, I know

And when she dedicates her song
And when her poem comes along
And you sift through the trash for the one you threw away

In your mental, maybe in time
Your changing heart will make it mine
And your plan will be to keep me
For at least
Another day.

Abril, Mil Novicientos Ochenta Y Tres

I would have slept on that sofa corner I didn't want to lay between them I knew what he wanted she sat on the edge of the bed talkin' through whoever was willing not to listen I listened to the sad bulging black eyes sitting outside the long-faced short kinky crown to understand those bulges locked in space I'd like to be where she was most times I knew what he wanted pre-teen breasts slightly fuzzy nature that learned early familiar with its own fingers and others and others and others I was sleepin' for real I felt those middle-aged fingers gently play with her she betrayed me I knew I shouldn't like it she betrayed me and she told my flesh that it had no control and she told my emotions to put their hands over my mouth and part my legs so he could I knew he was he said he was I didn't mean to like it at four she knew what she liked at thirteen she controlled me lord I just wanted a meal and maybe some lunch money fingers to the left of me tossed salad to the right soundlessly not knowing her hubby with his fingers in my soundlessly not knowing her hubby with his fingers in my I just wanted a meal I didn't mean to like it shoulda beat him 'til his pacemaker stopped there wasn't nothin' in the 'fridge at home shoulda emptied his spit can on his face and mommy's check don't come 'til next month shoulda I can't go to school tomorrow they'll smell fingers and throbbing and wet and silence

Nina Simone

Today I drown in nina simone finally I become myself oppression fails and I come to know leaves of a tree that don't grow here from seeds not planted that's what they said I was they looked into virgin eyes and blindly whispered you're nothing and they raped me from within fingers climbed exploring boney legs and knobby knees to unlock chastity and rape me from without planting the fear of loving myself loving only with tongues in hidden places and dances in dark places and touches in forbidden places creating a whore
a gratis
a gratis
a gratis
I never meant to need pain to survive
nina simone cries and moans for me her deep-bellied croons wrenching sweet tears faithful to my pride they hide and weep secretly under blankets of honesty under temporal escape longing to rise up and kill the master master the killer bum rush the bob wire that keeps them from me make a mad dash for my heart and give my cheeks a much needed bath I need to feel you stabbing me with your untruths and your deceit and your fake dreams and those b.s. promises of tomorrow
choking me
and
making me
need
pain to survive
nina bleeds for me her man's gone I let her touch me where I dream he plays lyrics lavishing my soul I orgasm while I pretend he tells me lies no desire to be free it tastes so good him hurting me going down I swallow the bitter thickness it burns I open to take more it burns searing what remains it burns I live for the heat behind my eyes as I replay him walking away from me and coming back to rob me some more of me pulling from me I downed forty pills for him and vomited for him and hallucinated for him

became a statistic for him I love you hating me consuming me stealing me
I know you need me, too
need pain
to survive
nina's howling an ever present scene me bathing in oils of regrets and i-wish-i-hads and if I could do it again I would kill those who stole from me I am a flower I am a fruitful tree my spiritual gifts raining down seeping into healthy ground penetrating roots of a good thing growing I am a flower I grow unnoticed by those who have eyes but cannot see and ears but cannot hear me sucking this phallus—this erection of soulful lies that I believed for the first twenty-five years of my life telling me you're nothing raping me from within fingers climbing exploring shapely legs and scuffed up knees freed from chastity and raping me from without fertilizing the fear of loving myself loving only with tongues . . . . and dances . . . . and . . . . forbidden . . . . killing a whore
a gratis
a gratis
a gratis
needing pain
nina simone girl—one who listens carefully breaks me knows me opens me holds me wipes tears that won't show erasing pain that won't go living lies breathing sighs hearing goodbyes die for me revive the child they buried alive in me chasing demons finding reasons to live in me freeing me saving me I hit the volume as she consumes me makes room in me for loving me filling me killing the need for pain in me
my man's gone now, ain't no use listenin' for his tired footsteps climbin' up the stairs[32] . . .
nina
sucked into the groove of my agony
needin' sad songs to stand
needin' lies to push on
needin' tears to breathe

---

[32] From *My Man's Gone Now* by Nina Simone

My Sister Doesn't Cry

My sister doesn't cry
her tears are like prisoners doin' life
in solitary, on death row, steel bars hold tight behind her eyes
but some once in a while
a brief moment arises
and a hearty laugh . . . a chuckle
makes like keys to the cell block
incites a prison riot . . . a jailbreak
and the few that escape scurry towards freedom
never looking back at the ones who didn't make it . . .

one time
she wuz crying
she wanted to go home
it teed me off
i barely gave her the time of day
she should've been thrilled to hang with
me

that must've been the day she packed away her pain
the key is in a safe deposit box in a bank vault
in her safe place
that nobody knows

but we're older now
and we've found a place together
forever's darkness is not this time
and time's not gonna make me forget no more
cuz i remember when flesh controlled me
cuz we were taught to hate each other by the things we saw
it's real easy to do when love don't know you

i'm glad we found out on our own
we have fresh new beginnings
and even though
my sister doesn't cry
she keeps smiles in her head from some long lost exultingly joyful jubilee
and she's not stingy with her smiles
and the package comes with tears

A Flower In The Snow

". . . Mysterious though it is, the characteristics in human nature which we love best grow in soil with a strong mixture of troubles."

Harry Emerson Fosdick
1878-1969, American Minister

She takes time to labor for love
Not really her own
Sacrificing all she has
Before she's really grown

Ignorance engulfs the children
So they don't even fear it
But the guillotine is intercepted
By the Holy Spirit

She was just as young as they
In her sub-developed mind
She couldn't see the pic'nees fall
And she was losing time

She would lose one on the way
The demons tried to snatch one away
One accomplished what they did not know
One was a flower in the snow

Captured by her mother's essence
A destiny to fail
Saved by minor differences
Blazing her own trails

She sees light where darkness lies
A blessing or a curse?
Excuses for the countless abuses
She forgets Who should come first

The love she gave was not real
She did not love herself
Took some time to look for "she"
Inside somebody else

Much to the enemies' dismay
Her Father's gone and made a way
Once buried neck-deep by her foe
She's the flower in the snow

There's an epidemic on
Oozing no self-esteem
Chokehold on the newborn goals
Suffocating some crisp-fresh dreams

Tearing through communities
Taking out in bubonic fashion
But The Blood was on her lentil
So it had to keep on passin'

Blindly walkin' in her grace
Mercy clothed her back
Steppin' in and out of mess
Her spirit still intact

She had to open up one day
The pain that she had stored away
Weeds around began to grow
To choke the flower in the snow

Contrary to popular belief
She's made it out alive
The struggle commences, she won't give in
Pre-destined to survive

Reconstructed appetite
Reconstructed mind
Born anew in Christ, our Savior
She is the perfect find

Detached from the transport vessel
He used to bring her out
Curses of the greats and grands
Denounced and cancelled out

She's the one that got away
Though she doesn't see it every day
This here's one Love she won't let go
Thus blooms a flower in the snow.

Pity Party

She just left her last pity party y'all
An' they keep bankin' on her fall
Even her friends got her marked for defeat
But she's a winner they don't know
For sure
She's go this beat

She's been diggin' chocolate since before it was fashionable
Her friends an' dem
They'd be in the gym
And they'd be giggin' on her
Cuz her new boo
Was deeper than midnight blue
He complimented her banana peel
Made her feel like she was the baddest chick on the planet
Sweatin' her like cats be diggin' Janet
Through the thickness of her glasses
When she got dissed
He saw past it
He treated her like a queen

One of a few on the scene wit' big boobies at the age of ten
She should known
It was blown
When the b-cups real quick-like became d's
Sportin' no bra and tight tees
She was destined to be somebodies' babies' mama
And through the drama
Mama never said a word
If she loved her
She never heard

She watched with her back turned
And her eyes closed
Did her conscience burn?
She acted like she didn't know
That by that time
There were many hands
Many tongues
Many selfish ones
Stay tuned
There's more to come

Uncle D tried to get some when she was only four
She watched the sun blazin' through the window caressin' his back
The demons in his eyes as he made his attack
Big, black penis caked with Vaseline
And Keri lotion
Hard pushes and jabbin' motions
By the grace of God he couldn't get it in
He couldn't get it in
Who knew he would open the door to her sin?
Her cervix became a sounding board
Her navel—a cup for semen
Shoulda been a lesbian
One brotha tried to git her to do her friend
She wasn't down wit' it
But somebody snuck one in
You see
She had her eyes closed
I mean
Her legs open
An' she was hopin' to feel some manhood pumpin' below her waist
But when she opened her eyes
There was a hotbox in her face
She didn't like the taste

So she has a hard time stayin' focused when she sees a handsome face
A hard jaw
Chiseled arms
Guess lookin' couldn't do no harm

If she wasn't the one lookin'
Her loins cookin' while you spittin' them lyrics
An' you ain't said a thing about sex
There's somethin' about a man wit' intellect
A man wit' talent
Self-respect
Hey, as long as he's breathin' she finds herself needin' to accomplish something
That's gon' leave her lookin' for someone else to bless
A new dingaling
To git wit'
Shoulda been a drug addict
But she was too busy trickin' for free
To smoke or pop or shoot or snort
Life is real short
She bases it on what she can see

Hmmmmmm?!?—wonder what they call people like she
Don't really matter cuz she gon' be who she gon' be
She holds her head up
And she sticks her chest out
And she stares straight ahead
Another sore spot in her heart
Another wet spot in her bed
Dealin wit' knuckleheads
Stalkin' her an' talkin' smack
Blind-sided by the nana-whoopin' they ain't know that honey packed
An' they keep comin'
But she's drummin' to the beat of a new dance
One more chance to let go
Clingin' to dysfunction cuz it's all she really knows
Confessed the Lord
Professin' freedom
Still findin' it hard to grow
Cuz the drummer want some
And the preacher
Can't even trust her teacher
So she keeps doin' her do

But this time
She figured
She'd try somethin' new
She stopped blamin' her mama for the things she didn't do
She forgave the less-thans that played wit' her innocence
And her mind
When she was growin' up
Where death kept showin' up
And she didn't know the time
These days she finds
It's much easier to just
Let it go
And she knows
That her son will be a strong man
Even with no man around
And her daughter won't be a ho' cuz her mommy let her down
An'
As soon as she finds herself
Content chillin' by herself
Then comes that one
That bold blessing
Like life just begun
Who will gaze upon her bareness
And not mistake her kindness
For naiveté
He will use his spirit-man
And stroke her in a better way
Find out where she really hides

An' even though she still can't help wonderin' how you ride
She'll just smile at you
An' keep all her feelin's inside
Honey's still young
But she understands
And she's not tryin' to taint another man
She knows that you can be broken
Just like she
Her intention is always to deal wit' honesty

Still it seems like everything these days makes her horny
And this corny phase she's pushin' through
In another day or two
She'll forget about you
In the meantime
She buries it all
And when she gits home
She'll take it out on her live-in booty call

She just left her last pity party y'all
An' they keep bankin' on her fall
Even her friends got her marked for defeat
But she's a winner they don't know
For sure
She's got this beat.

Little Girl

For Ché La The Mehlodi

Always scared at first
Can't pinpoint the worst
But, you get used to it
Cuz it's all the same, it
Becomes a way of life
Bringing the same pain, same strife
Something you come to expect
Teaching you self-disrespect

Hey! Be quiet—shoosh!
You fresh, untampered puss
I guess that's the true thrill
Taken against your will
Too young to fight, so you lay
Let the men have their play
Pray to wake from this bad dream
Nowhere to run—but inside your scream

How come you don't cry?
Why won't your spirit die?
Why do you never tell?
And your heart has no hard shell?
How is it that, all the while
You still find a way to smile?
To where disappears your fear?
Why do you still want them here?

You can't understand
Why even with your own hands
You continue the pattern
And you take what you've learned
And you practice it on yourself
Have you been tainted, or have the helped?
Has it made your person better?
Or are you messed up altogether?

They soiled your mind, your youth, your flesh
When your cookies weren't even cookies yet
They selfishly tasted of what they had no right
And you still take it to bed with you at night
It's interfering with your plans
And you can't even keep a man
Cuz the haunting doesn't quit
And you don't think you'll survive this

Strong child, I hear you
And I will always be near you
Will you give some of your tears to me?
I know from where it is you want to flee
I know that, as soon as you're packed
The memories, they always pull you back
In your quest for free, for peace of mind
You fall behind; you—fall—behind

Don't stress it, move on
Let the past be gone
Don't stress it, let it by
You'll come to know the reasons why
Use that pain to stand upon
To make you bigger, wiser, strong
Cuz I know there's nothing you want more in this world
Than one more shot at being a little girl.

¿Hasta El Fuego?

"... but while she was still a long way off, her father saw her and was filled with compassion for her; he ran to his daughter, threw his arms around her and kissed her."

Luke 15:20(emphasis added)

I can't wait til later
Cuz later's already been
And I've struggled up to now
To fight evils within

And He told me yesterday
As He tells me everyday
His admonitions clearly said
It was gonna be this way

He told me, yes He did
About the rains, that they would cease
But he also said the fires
The fires would release

So I prepare to leave
For in that I can be free
And there's no luggage to retrieve
Cuz all He wants is me

Please don't you say later
Cuz later's not really yours
You'd best be gettin' ready
For your sake and for the cause

Too many times in yesterday
As too many times today
The door was open and chance was there
For you to change your way

And he knows you very well
So when the rains have ceased
Will you know him any better
Before the fires release

And will you then believe
The one love that is true
Will you open and receive
The love he has for you?

Remembering (Holding On Part 2)

I just need you to hold me
Please don't let go
Hold me until I don't feel you anymore

I just wanna stay right here
Joy endures for a night
But weeping comes in the morning
So, tonight, please
Just hold me like you love me
Like you never said you were fine without me
Like you know you need me
Like you can see who I really am
Pretend for me
Make those tears that come-easy when I'm trying to leave you
I know they're not for me
You are feeling
And feelings aren't love
But I really don't care
Ha-ha . . . I really don't care

Please don't let go
Just
Hold me until I don't feel you
Anymore.

They Said

"In the same way, was not even Rahab the prostitute considered righteous . . . ?"

James 2:25 (NIV)

They said that I was sleepin' so I didn't really know
They said cuz I was sleepin' that it wouldn't really show
They said since I was sleepin' that I didn't know the way
I'm wide awake, so tell me, y'all, what am I to say?

They said that I was lost so I could not take the blame
The said cuz I was lost that my sin was not the same
They said since I was lost that I did not let Him down
So tell me, please, what do I do now that I am found?

They said that I was bound so I couldn't do it right
They said cuz I was bound that I couldn't really fight
They said since I was bound my spirit could not get loose
So now that I have been untied, what is my excuse?

They said that I was blind cuz they didn't raise me well
They said cuz I was blind that I really couldn't tell
They said since I was blind that I really couldn't be
So tell me how I work it now, now that I can see?

When JC Comes

We ride together in the dimness
Protected only by vanilla candlelight flicker
Absorbing us
Leaving only silhouettes
We glow
And I plant my pleasures into you
Your lips say strange familiar things
You try to suck back all the fire that escapes from you
Softly I scream my enjoyment
And gently tear the darkness with utterances of another's name
Oh, God
Oh, Jesus
Oh, Lord
And you roll in the sounds
And you add your own pleas
For mercy
In an instant, the darkness is rent by burning light
I can't look in
But I know
This light
There's no time to scream now
No time to plea
For mercy
Snatched by this fire
And my in-obeisance
Slowly melting in my regret
I don't even know what
Happened to you
All I know is that the fires here
Don't stop being fires
No embers, no ashes
Only now do I remember somebody askin' me what I wanted to be doin'
when he comes again.

Black Sunday Dawning

A new girl, she was in the mix
My feelings in her eyes
I was the one to play the tricks
While she concealed my lies

A sweet fate I thought best ignored
Only speaking through her pace
Sure that I had finally scored
I gave my fear her face

I dipped my middle finger in it
It went straight to my head
My conscience tried its best to thin it
But my backside hugged the bed

She stayed before my closed up eyes
She closed up her eyes before me
Still she held onto my lies
Quiet promise to keep them for me

I never saw that I could see
When she told me I could go
Tonight, she allowed me to be
And she didn't let them know

I think that I was brave for her
Her strength, too, puffed me up
She and I, we did concur
We'd overflowed our cup

Hers was filled with cappuccino
Mine, to the brim with wine
Neither one cast out the mellow
Or made us draw the line

If I could kill-off my emotions
Mutilate them one by one
She'd only come in her devotion
And give me back the sun

The new girl—new even to the tricks
With her own special brand of lies
She made the transfer in the mix
Left me feeling through her eyes

Leeches suck a fruitless find
As we're swept into the gyrus
I know right now her heart is mine
Cuz I lost mine in her iris

Rebirth of a Sista

Anabasis [ê-'næ-bê-sis]—(noun)—A movement upward or forward, as a military advance; the antonym of "retreat."

My mom seemed blind to it, she couldn't teach me much
With regards to who I am, my significance and such
So I grew up shadowed by ignorance, a little out of touch
No real connection with my culture

Yet slowly but surely I've begun to reach the peak
And whenever I open up and part my lips to speak
Out comes a mind that surpasses those of the weak
Cuz now I can fight off the vultures

Parasitic in nature, robbing the mind
If I do not allow it they will not find
What promotes the fortitude of my kind
Cuz they only want to break it down

Silently I lay back and observe the ploy
Their so-thought covert mission of seek and destroy
Little do they know, I have a decoy
And I refuse to be bound

They smile at me and think that I don't know
Why poverty and death in my community grows
I know in whose pockets the capital flows
But I also know who really has the power

My child, my mother, my sister, my brother
We have to build what it takes to kill the killing amongst each other
Let it be known we won't be silenced, we won't be smothered
We will hold onto what is ours

Why should I ask permission of somebody else
To own a freedom that already belongs to myself?
I will press up till they 'fess up; my presence will be strongly felt
I'll haunt their dreams; they will be shaken

The young of my flesh depend upon my non-submission
To these demons set on a common mission
Forever bent on a Christian race omission
But my Spirit will not be taken.

Who Knows

I live for when we cry cuz we happy
an' our hearts bleed into one

there'd be nothing to wish, for me, it'd be a new day
an' I think i'd be havin' fun

this season brings a new thing to fruition
an' it won't make us flip out

we'll learn to keep it steady
we'll learn to kill the doubt

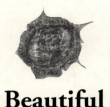

Beautiful

Beautiful
Often, her spirit moves me
Not knowing—yet, knowing
She evokes the tears I treasure so
But, joy is their origin
Radiating comfort
Freedom
Peace

You see,
Her heart—it tells me stories
Her heart—it tells my stories
No longer grim with pain
A real smile in her eyes
That I receive
Even before it travels and arrests her entire face
My sister
My sister
My Father—MY GOD
Thank You for making her so
Thank You for making us so
Beautiful.

January 2009 (Random Thought 1)

There was blood on the sidewalk this morning
On 8th Avenue between 130th and 131st
It was almost fresh; not yet brown
Blotches began near the garbage piles
They got smaller
They zig-zagged
They trailed off in the middle of the sidewalk
Once-small puddles had begun to seep into the concrete

Men with jobs are a hot commodity again
They can make promises they don't have to keep
New babies' mamas will settle for make-believe love and EBT cards

There was a conversation on a crowded #2 train
He talked like he was in his own living room
But he wasn't
My four—and seven-year-old daughters stood feet below as he loudly proclaimed a close shave
Yo, I almost had another baby's momz
She got her period and I said, Word? Good. Cuz I ain't effin' wi'choo no more.
He kept talking while his friend and all the rest of us tuned in against our will

I remember what I used to think of the welfare mother
I had a degree in bourgeoisie ghetto princess
It got me in the front door
But it was enough to build a throne upon
I came crashing down on HRA's doorsteps
Three times

I walked by again and the stains were gone
The snow-melted-turned to ice-melted-snow and ice again washed as if it had never been
You can paint the town whatever color you want
But the pain is in the walls
The blood of the ones who brought the acceptable sacrifice cries out from the concrete

The Condition of My Body As I Try Not to Lose My Mind (Random Thought 2)

I wrote this as I was finding out that yet another challenge had come a-knockin': Lupus. My body had been alluding to it for years; the official diagnosis came in July 2009.

The pain has not yet come
But I can feel the throbbing
I lie perfectly still
And it's like a second heartbeat

I saw two people on the corner
A man and a woman
They were laughing
She was feeding him with her fingers
Years of drug abuse was on their faces
But love was in their eyes

I don't care what position I choose
My back still hurts when I move
This could take years to complete
A random thought, pages long
So many things going on
My handwriting growing again

Sometimes I find it hard to love
Sometimes I question the stories of old
There is no question of Who You Are
But there is always the possibility that I might be crazy
As my hair becomes more brittle and thin in the middle
And my vision blurs
I take the time at least to line my eyes with amethyst
I am still beautiful as I contemplate shaving my head
It's a little flat in the back

I am disconnecting from the lies that stuck
I wish I knew for sure
Spring will come with answers, I pray
Decisions
Maybe I will let go
I feel the bald patches in the middle of my head
I'm too young for this
But I know there's grace for this
I will learn to cry in the dark
The tears will fly like wind's dandelions
The tears will fly like butterflies psychedelic
The tears will fly like fireflies
And I will still have a smile when the sun comes
I am learning complete surrender
You should never put stipulations on your deliverance
God is not afraid to give you what you want
You should never put stipulations on your peace

I will have given my mind over
It will be found in the Right Place
I will have given my will over
It will be found in a Good Place
I will have given my emotions over
They will be found serving a purpose
You pay for this freedom everyday . . .

Not-Life, Death, & the Resurrection
For Shoni

I almost threw it all away
I had every opportunity to escape
But I stayed there
Buck naked amidst strangers
Truth or dare was mostly dares and I had no business being so daring
And so untruthful
So stupid
I love you
I wished he would stop saying that
How badly did I want someone?

A very dangerous game I played with men who did not love themselves
My self-esteem was throne and they were king of my very soul
They sat and ruled and judged and smiled
While I fell to pieces
I am no anomaly
You know it all too well
It is thick and dark and strangle-holds you in a place that keeps you groveling and begging even though they won't budge.
You let them enter you and deposit into you and take out of you
You can't help yourself
Because you have great hope
Faith in the unseen although the unseen can't be found in what you hope for
You keep pushing until something breaks
You risk losing everything
Your very life belongs to them and all it takes is you reaching out and pulling it back in
You would rather fall
You would rather die than be alone

You cry and someone hears
Someone knows that you would give your life for True Love
You would take black-and-blues for True Love for as long as you had to
And you do
You take them until you die
And when you die
Finally there's the other side
You are in the water and you are swimming
You are flowing through clear blue waters
You are surrounded by beautiful fish and coral and water things that don't bite or choke or electrocute
They seem to smile at you and welcome you as you flow
As you submit to the gentle pull
Your eyes are 20/20 and you are smiling
And there's light above the waters
Light pulls you up above
And you see the other side

And you know that, on the other side, it doesn't matter what comes
Because you know you can't go back to where you were
You know that, on this side, there is a throne
But it's not your self-esteem
There is smiling
But it's not because you are in pain
There is an entering and a deposit and a taking out
But the entering is salvation
And the deposit is true love
And the taking out is all that they gave you that you did not need
And you are free
You are so free and you know it and you can't stop crying because it is so good
True love collects your new tears so that when you forget
Because you will forget
They will be there for you to remember
You will remember when you died and the waters brought you through
And you'll live again.

Child of The King (Chosen One)

she's at it again
the chosen one
flew beyond sight
almost hit the sun

downward spiral
eclipsed her none
see the corona?
she's a chosen one

she'll pick up
she'll pick up

she's no
fallen angel

climbin' demons
surround the place
she stands firm
with stoic face

sometimes a smile
to trick the masses
the chosen one
recovers fastest

nasty bruise
came from the fall
she will make it
after all

gave her life
to The Risen One
she was chosen
her job's not done

ella tiene miedo
but she can't run
she's locked in
a chosen one

a special breed
dem can't outrun
destined for heaven
chosen one.

To Love (A Song)

On fire again
Faces that façade joy and courage and strength parade before my eyes
Eyes that want to remain closed because
It was so easy to ignore where I'd been before
But these faces
With sinister grins
Profanity spewing lips
And haunting eyes
They scream
Please come and get me
Take me out of me
Help me to love

Convicted
Again
Bodies posturing menace and brick walls and imperviousness before I pass by
Wanting to pass by because
It was so easy to say that's not my concern
But these bodies
With marks and holes
Obscenities exposed
They groan
Please come and get me
Take me out of me
Help me to love

From the same cloth
Same tree
Same fertile ground
That He made me

Is the one who runs
from the
Whoop-whoop
Fires the
Pop-pop
Smokes the
Sssssssss

But he's mine
She's mine
Just two short steps
From doing time
I am
Not so far removed that I can't feel the groove that compels them to pursue
What
Doesn't
Work
Only
Brings
Hurt

Turned around, again
Spirits crying lonely and hungry and if only in my soul
Soul that knows it's my war, too
Cuz these spirits
With similar image
They bellow
Please come and get me
Take me out of me
Help me to love
They bellow
Please come and get me
Take me out of me
Help me to love
Help me to love
Help me to love
Help me to love . . .

Shelter

"Give me a reason. Because, if you don't, I'm leaving. I didn't sign up for this."

I was sifting through a storage bin. Looking for more stuff to throw away. Again. There was no room for anything, so I was sifting. Sifting through my life. Looking for more stuff . . .

We were living in a one-room apartment in a Tier II shelter, to accommodate a family of five. Bunk this. I'm done. There's my old green date book. And an envelope marked "Him." I opened the envelope and removed the folded sheet of yellow legal paper. At the top was written "My Husband." The date next to it was March 19, 1999.

On this piece of paper—this list that I had written in 1999 when I was single and promiscuous and holding men responsible for my confusion and angry with God—was my destiny. I had written him down and put him away and forgotten about him; right up to the moment I was planning to leave him. The reason jumped off the paper and assaulted my eyes; assaulted my spirit with conviction and repentance: In love with the Lord . . . a good driver . . . loves my children as his own . . .

There is so much more in the man than was on the paper. What I had been looking at was not what was. He was set aside—sanctified for me. A sigh. A revelation. Another offering of my portion of the gift of humility. I put the paper away and cleaned out the bin; slowly while God cleaned out my heart . . .

Para Mi Domi

I want to get you right
Recite you like the poetry that lets me live
Get to know me, so I can show up right
When you turn around and realize that you picked up the wrong package

There are things I haven't seen
Some ways that I haven't stumbled upon
You bloom a little more, and the seeds you disperse when wind blows bring color
And scent
And new life

I know that
When I show you me
You might want to close your eyes and rewind me to try to hear something else
I like that about you
I worry about using you up
And the truth being something different from what I know
Am I really me?
Surely we've both been shaken

The unfamiliar brings us closer
But it tells you to keep an eye on me
And tells me to look over my shoulder and ride in reverse
But there's no place to return to

Yes, I know, when I get full I talk in riddles
Even I don't understand
But you loved the frail, broken girl-woman
You held her, even half-believing
When she had long since given up on you

Hands clung tightly
To familiarity and death
And found familiarity and death writhing to get away
Thank God

Now
We break together
And the shards fall upon each other
And we make a new pane
And we can see all the way through.

Friendly Fire

He comes in, and I feel an internal embrace. Eruptions occur all over the place—enveloping my entireness, burning through my flesh; charring my sole soul—and I could desire no less.

He sweeps through me—I like this kinda burnin'—cracklin', turn up the heat on my pulse—all the more I be yearnin'. Engulfed in His flames, I am melted to the bone; there, where the hold He has on me is eminently shown.

I scream—OH!—pleasure pain—can it get any higher? I bathe in the heat, consumed by His friendly fire.

Loving U

Then came blankets of snow
U were calling again
Sheets of white
Curtained my window pane
Your heart reached out & said
I'm loving U

Imagination swept up
& twined us 2
& all that happy
has buried U
at least 6'
deep up inside of me

U say come outside
so we can B wet
all drenched in us
all soaked in kismet
flurries hitting making quiet touch making me
loving U

Strange Connection
For Che' La The Mehlodi

I was really young when I felt this
Shouldn't have known the things that I did
But, the lessons started early on
And later on, when I learned to hide

The problems started to grow
I ran out of space to hide my woes
And so the smile that had been my mask
And the laughter that drowned the pain

Were overcome by a build-up of grief
And now's the time that I find my relief
And I know that I've found it some
In the friend I have in you

It's not my fault—you got me open
And, I was kinda thinkin'—hopin'
That maybe you'd stick around for a while
Maybe you would like to chill

It's okay now, I think I can deal
I'm in the company of somebody real
And I don't need you to hold me up
But, help lift me when I fall

And when your hidin' space gets too tight
And you've just about had it with life
Let your peripheral pull you to
—to the left, to the right and all around
Guess who?!?

Strange as can be, and don't care who knows
Just so long as the strange in you shows
Now I know just how we connect
'Cause I'm strange, too

And when I smile and your eyes smile back
I know for sure you've always got my back
And I don't sweat tomorrow
'Cause I've got today with you.

The Best Love Yet (Para Mi Domi Part 2)

We did not have the flashing lights
The explosions & sparks that happen when Tom kisses the she-cat in my fave childhood animations
No butterflies or blushing

Our assurance came through a knowing
Our love was God-kissed before the sky & the seas, the evening & the day, green life & four-leggers, swimmers & flyers & creeping things

We took roads that broke us, wore us out & made us give up
And we were replaced with who we were to be
Then we met "we" & it all made sense
Then battles raged as old "us" fought to reclaim its place-now-lost & found no place to rest

And after each battle we found ourselves closer
Tighter
Wounded but willing
We picked each other up
We bonded

And now we have flashing colored lights everyday
POP! BOOM! ZIP!
Big beautiful butterflies that never die
Solid rooted love that does not break barriers, but blows them to pieces

I love the love stories of "At first sight" & "It's always been you"
But I revel in the drama
The dynamics
The adventure of a broken love put back together where it should have been when it was born

I think that's the best love story yet

Misty

I stepped outside today and found a pretty grey sky
There was mist and warmth
And the ground was wet with after-rain

And they all complained of fog
They cursed the dampness and the darkness of the day
But all I could see was you

A water that grows things like hope and promise
A sultry sky bringing reasons to come close and stay put

You live in me
Shhh—listen
I'll let the rain tell it
Let the clouds speak my peace to you

It ain't so easy
Seein' the good in rain
But I'll put away my umbrella and let you shelter me

I look up and see a smiling face
Smokey eyes and weeping-tears of joy
I hug myself while the rest run for cover

They stare at me cuz I smile when I walk
My clothes cling to me
My feet squoosh in my shoes

Water drips from my hair into my eyes
I blink back the stinging sensation
And stroll on with my thoughts

I can actually feel you touching me in my visions of you
It's all so pure and clean
Like new love you hold me and make me yours

All I did was step outside today
And you came pouring down on me with that rain . . .

I Forgot To Tell You Somethin'

Love is you, and I ain't livin' another life

    I forgot to tell you somethin', the last time when I lay with you, Honey skin wrapped in Cocoa skin, hands entwined, drinking love from your eyes, I discovered who I really was
    He made you for me, when I was still just trying to be, I'm glad I found I'm someone for you
    It was hard to crawl from under the skeletons I dug up
    What kept me from you is what keeps me lovin' you

Love is you, and I ain't livin' another life

    As you lay here touching me, like you' got a now&later cooled after sittin' on a radiator, the thin wax paper clings relentlessly to what's left of its square-ness, you peel me delicately, you savor the fragile melting me, the intensified aroma of candy essence you softly dissolve to a tangy aftertaste, a colorful mat remains, and the scent of sweet fruit
    Sweet fruit is what I'll make with you, each day another layer is shed and I WANT TO LOVE YOU
    Smitten
    Driven by the sadness in your voice when you smile, the smile in your eyes when you cry, the trust in your pulse when you touch me and pull me into you

Love is you, and I ain't livin' another life

    Your kiss right now is killng me; not the me that you need, but the me that says that you're not real, the me that tells my soul you're gonna change me and leave me to die

You're killing me right now; not the me that loves you, but the me that says you'll destroy my dreams, the me that tells my heart you'll go past dejection and stomp my spirit to pieces, leaving nothing

Here's the me comin' that knows that you're the man

Glad I didn't go past waiting, glad you stayed waiting so that healing made us free and

The way you're holding me right now becomes a fragment of what our time in this place will be

Love is you,
And I ain't livin'
Another life.

Hearing from God

So
Outside my window
I look up and see the packing tape
That was used to patch up the headlight
On the left side of the old
Dirty
White nissan
It's detaching itself
One end of it blowing in the wind
Waving in the sun
Dancing reflections on my window pane
They play a one-sided round of run catch and kiss
With the crayon scratchings and the scuff marks
And the dirty hand prints on my bedroom wall
So
I'm trying to hear from God
I think I open my heart
Search for what I can identify
And tip it over and pour it into His lap
The stuff that sticks to the bottom won't shake loose
I tap it on the bottom
I say "thank you"
And "in Jesus' name"
And "amen"
And I listen
And the phone rings
And I strap on my attitude
Cuz I think it's "him" calling to apologize
But "him" hangs up before the machine responds
So
I listen

The phone, again
One time—hang up
I listen
The day's upcoming events plug my ears
So
I get up
But I can't tell if I hear anything
So
I
Listen
And my eyes catch the reflections
Of those pretty flickers
From the dirty tape
Clinging to that broken headlight
And
Trying to escape in the wind.

This Simple Melody

I hope this a for-real thing
This swarm that's stingin' me
The atmosphere of you alive and rising
From this
Simple melody

I never thought a plain ol' love song could sway me
I close my eyes and go about my night
I bend
I let it play me

I fight to keep you out my sleep
But the battle's lost and my heart receives the pang
Prayin' that I'm not rollin' into another plain ol' love thang

Can you help me understand why I'm suddenly broken pieces?
This new mellow that's buggin' me
Tuggin' me
And
Got me callin' Jesus?

Each day in bits and pieces you take my resolve
Like sugar granules they fall into your water and dissolve

I think I like this
This art of painting me a picture anew
An enamored fool—a smitten kitten, bitten
Fittin' likin' becomin' a lover of you

Taking my fears between your fingers and tearing them to shreds
Casting them to the wind with the doubt you snatched from my head

I hope this is a for-real thing
This swarm that's stingin' me
The atmosphere of you alive and rising
From this
Simple melody

If I Was Blind

If I was blind, I'd still know you're beautiful
Without hands, I could still touch your fire
If my lips could not experience yours
I'd still know of their softness
And I'd taste the sweetness
Of the organ that shapes your words

My ears, with no ability to interpret sound
Could still hear you speak
Cuz, when you speak
All senses respond without consent

If I were to die tomorrow
You would for ALWAYS live inside of me
And when my spirit possessed its next life
It would emit all that is you
And a new world would reap your glory

If never had we met
I know that, in some way
Our souls would be acquainted
For the grass that meets your feet
And the wind that grazes your skin
When I meet them, they pass on the blessings
Of the knowledge of you

I will always be happy to see you
But, if I was blind
I would still know
That you are beautiful.

With Me (Para Mi Domi, Part 3)

There's a kiss that goes deep
There's a touch that bonds skin
There's a look that unites hearts
There's a love that you can see
I need you to have that with me

Every part that connects
Holds
Builds life
Can I chase away the things that make you hide inside?
Can I give you all of me?
May I please?

Remember when you said
You wanted to wrap yourself in me?
We're still pushin' into one
And it hasn't yet become
The years were thieves
The past was lies
We've lived in them so long
We see through blurry eyes

I'm watching you
While a blizzard blows between
If we could find those two
The he before the pain
The she before the stains

I know that I would find myself
Listening to you call my name
Crying like I did when your love produced the rain
Bold like when I found out who I am

If not forever
But just one time before you go
I'd like for us to know
I'd really like to show

All the things I would have saved
If I had known you would come
You are the song that I sang so long
You are the song
You are the song

I know there's more and we will have it
Sweet fantasy/memory/reality/dream
Our healing is together
If only I could say it clear
If I could make your spirit hear
You would come near

You would come open
You would rise to my kiss that goes deep
You would yield to my touch that bonds skin
You would weep into my look that unites hearts
You would fall into my love that you can see
You would have that with me

The End

There are some stories left untold.
Sometimes words run out.
They come back again.

As I end this, it is eight-24s into a dark day. I have found that I have lupus. My family is disconnecting from the place we had come to call home. And the thing I feared more than illness that does not end, more than injury that incapacitates or the permanency of death—the thing that ought not be—has crept upon my beautiful little ones; all of them.

My heart wants to implode—I want to hurt people—the tenderness is so deep. But their father's tears bind us and promise a day when nothing alien or familiar will break our cohesion.

My spirit still knows The One Who redeemed and healed me from the places I've been, and I know that this deepest gray that my family now endures will be whitest snow when these night tears fade to morning joy.

See you on the other side.[33]

---

[33] If you are living with some form of abuse, please, please, please tell someone. Don't keep it to yourself. It can kill you; and you are valuable and very much needed *alive*. I don't need to know you personally to know that. Please see the resources in the back of this book for ways to get help. I bid you peace in the Name of Jesus Christ.

Statistics on Sexual Abuse

About Victims

One in six women and one in thirty-three men will be a victim of sexual assault in their lifetime.
College-age women are four times more likely to be sexually assaulted.

Sexual Assault Numbers

In 2007, there were 248,300 victims of sexual assault.
Every two minutes, someone in the United States is sexually assaulted.

Reporting to Police

Approximately 60 percent of sexual assaults are not reported to the police.
Reporting has increased by one-third since 1993.

About Rapists

Approximately 73 percent of rape victims know their assailants.
Only 6 percent of rapists will ever spend a day in jail.

Statistics Surrounding Child Sexual Abuse

Prevalence is the percentage of the population that is affected by child sexual abuse; the general existence of child sexual abuse.
Consequence is the impact that child sexual abuse has on a victim/survivor and on our society over time.
Sexual abuse touches every life when it leads to losses of trust, decreases in self-esteem, and development of shame, guilt, and depression.
Sexual abuse touches every life when it leads to eating disorders, substance abuse, suicide, promiscuity/prostitution, and other psychobehavioral issues.
The statistics are shocking
One in four girls is sexually abused before the age of eighteen.
One in six boys is sexually abused before the age of eighteen.
One in five children are solicited sexually while on the Internet.
Nearly 70 percent of all reported sexual assaults (including assaults on adults) occur to children ages seventeen and under.
An estimated 39 million survivors of childhood sexual abuse exist in America today.
Even within the walls of their own homes, children are at risk for sexual abuse.
Around 30-40 percent of victims are abused by a family member.
Another 50 percent are abused by someone outside of the family whom they know and trust.
Approximately 40 percent are abused by older or larger children whom they know.
Therefore, only 10 percent are abused by strangers.
Sexual abuse can occur at all ages, probably younger than you think.
The median age for reported abuse is nine years old.
More than 20 percent of children are sexually abused before the age of eight.

Nearly 50 percent of all victims of forcible sodomy, sexual assault with an object, and forcible fondling are children under 12.
Most children don't tell even if they have been asked.
Evidence that a child has been sexually abused is not always obvious, and many children do not report that they have been abused.
Over 30 percent of victims never disclose the experience to *anyone*.
Young victims may not recognize their victimization as sexual abuse.
Almost 80 percent initially deny abuse or are tentative in disclosing. Of those who do disclose, approximately 75 percent disclose accidentally. Additionally, of those who do disclose, more than 20 percent eventually recant even though the abuse occurred.
Fabricated sexual abuse reports constitute only 1 percent to 4 percent of all reported cases. Of these reports, 75 percent are falsely reported by adults and 25 percent are reported by children. Children only fabricate 1/2 percent of the time.
Consequences of child sexual abuse begin affecting children and families immediately. They also affect society in innumerable and negative ways. These effects can continue throughout the life of the survivor so the impact on society for just one survivor continues over multiple decades. Try to imagine the impact of thirty-nine million survivors.

Health and/or Behavioral Problems:

The way a victim's family responds to abuse plays an important role in how the incident affects the victim.
Sexually abused children who keep it a secret or who "tell" and are not believed are at greater risk than the general population for psychological, emotional, social, and physical problems often lasting into adulthood.
Children who have been victims of sexual abuse are more likely to experience physical health problems (e.g., headaches).
Victims of child sexual abuse report more symptoms of PTSD, more sadness, and more school problems than nonvictims.
Victims of child sexual abuse are more likely to experience major depressive disorder as adults.
Young girls who are sexually abused are more likely to develop eating disorders as adolescents.
Adolescent victims of violent crime have difficulty in the transition to adulthood, are more likely to suffer financial failure and physical injury, and are at risk to fail in other areas due to problem with behaviors and outcomes of the victimization.

Drug and/or Alcohol Problems:

Victims of child sexual abuse report more substance abuse problems. Around 70-80 percent of sexual abuse survivors report excessive drug and alcohol use. Young girls who are sexually abused are three times more likely to develop psychiatric disorders or alcohol and drug abuse in adulthood, than girls who are not sexually abused.
Among male survivors, more than 70 percent seek psychological treatment for issues such as substance abuse, suicidal thoughts, and attempted suicide. Males who have been sexually abused are more likely to violently victimize others.

Teenage Pregnancy and Promiscuity:

Children who have been victims of sexual abuse exhibit long-term and more frequent behavioral problems, particularly inappropriate sexual behaviors. Women who report childhood rape are three times more likely to become pregnant before age eighteen.
An estimated 60 percent of teen first pregnancies are preceded by experiences of molestation, rape, or attempted rape. The average age of their offenders is twenty-seven years.
Victims of child sexual abuse are more likely to be sexually promiscuous. More than 75 percent of teenage prostitutes have been sexually abused.

Crime:

Adolescents who suffer violent victimization are at risk for being victims or perpetrators of felony assault, domestic violence, and property offense as adults.
Nearly 50 percent of women in prison state that they were abused as children.
Over 75 percent of serial rapists report they were sexually abused as youngsters.
Most perpetrators don't molest only one child if they are not reported and stopped.
Nearly 70 percent of child sex offenders have between one and nine victims; at least 20 percent have ten to forty victims.
An average serial child molester may have as many as four hundred victims in his lifetime.

Finding Healing

If you are in an emergency situation, get to a safe place, if you can, and dial 911 or your local precinct.

Tell a teacher, a close friend, a trusted adult. Abusers will make you think there's no one, but there is always someone willing to help.

Dial 311 and ask for resources for survivors of sexual abuse; there are *plenty*.

http://www.angelrockproject.com/arp/projects/10_signs_of_child_abuse.asp

E-mail me at bigheadedsista@gmail.com. I check it several times a day and I *always* answer personally. There's nothing too deep for me.

Much Gratitude and Thanks To

My Lord, there is nothing I want more in this life than to please You; You *are* my everything; You saw a big mess and cleaned it up just in time; I love you . . . I will die serving You . . . My beautiful husband, Pastor Dominic Lewis; even though we often got it wrong, we fought it out (and each other) until we got it right. No one else could have braved and overcome the challenges of marriage and parenthood and poverty and baby-mama-and-daddy-drama with me; no one else would I want on the front lines with me. Love with you is intense, passionate, and powerful; I'm glad it's you and me . . . My amazing son, Pastor Quentin Bernard Samuels; you loved me when I was crazy and feeding you Doritos, French onion dip, and Kool-Aid. The devil has permanent track marks from your psychedelic sneakers and the sneakers of your children to come; you will never be the tail . . . My vivacious daughters, Kevineh McFarland, Meeyah and Jucenia Lewis; vibrant, vivacious, in-your-face, and loving. You grow me up. I see pieces of me that I can love in each and every one of you . . . My brothers, Harold and Jessie, and my dad, Louis Bell—your time on this earth was so short, but I believe that you left something that caused me to go on and kick in doors. Say hello to Jesus for me; I love you so very much . . .

Aunt Jenice—because of you, I know Jesus for myself; thank you for praying for me all those years, thank you for letting your light shine before me and for not letting me get away with *anything* . . .

Aunt Delores—my Auntie-Pooh, my twin, my inspiration, my smile, my first glimpse of real love . . . you carried me through a really dark place and taught me how to stand . . .

Mommy—Harriette—you had no idea what you were getting into when you took me in, but I'm so glad you did; thank you for showing me what real love is . . .

My bestest friends in the whole world—Shoni (Trishon), ChaCha (Charmin), Mehlo (Michelle), Lisa (Liz), Jeanne (Nena) and 'Rhonda (LeRhonda, I'm sorry, I have no nickname for you); No one could have been what you've been to me; only if the Lord tells me will I ever let you go. I love you so very much . . .

Special Acknowledgments

My biological mom and sister, Edith and Nilda—glad we got a second chance; my other mothers, Tia Ceci, Carletta (dancin' in heaven), Ms. Westbury, Ms. Queenie; my sisters, Liz (Lisa), Nena (Jean'ne), Nilda, Yacey, Yvette, Sharon, Tyesh, Tasheis, DeVonni, and Keisha, Keisha S., Tasia (Stacy), Natasha and Shanelle, Break-The-Day (Dawn), Mary (I heard that), Jenni (*I love you, man*!), Tyescha, Myra, DeeDee, Heather, Joy, Gina, Kim; my children from another mother, Keren and Orlando; my too-old-to-be-stepchildren, Ryan and Troy; my nieces and nephew Shawanna, Ashley, William, Alyssa, Chayse, Kayla, and Autumn; my dear friends, Adrienne and Rebecca, I hope I make you proud . . .

There are so many people with whom I've experienced some part of life, who have also inspired these writings. Please don't hold me to listing all of you here. I have lived a lot—you'll forgive me if I forget. I appreciate you—each and every one of you—including those of you who meant me no good. I am more than blessed to have encountered you. Please know that I love you for the part you played in bringing me this far . . .

***And a special thanks to my amazing editor Carla Chapelle, who made me dig deeper (how brave of you, CC!), and to all the people who read some part of my book for me, including Trishon Crawford, Janet Avery, Mi Domi, Jenni Ginn, Mary Klausner, Heather Smith, Kim Emery, and Tony Chapelle—thank you for braving *las paginas de mi vida*; your advice, encouragement, and admonishment mean so much.

Peace

Bibliography

http://www.darkness2light.org/KnowAbout/statistics_2.asp

http://www.rainn.org/statistics

www.beyondabuse.com